"This is a book you'll want to underline and return to over and over again. Marriage is hard, and Becky Hunter, while being honest about its difficulties, has presented a clear and biblical plan that could radically transform your marriage. If you're looking for something to help you 'fix' your husband, this isn't your book. But if you are looking for God's way to live both as a 'present' to your husband and a powerful witness for Christ in the world, read *Being Good to Your Husband on Purpose*. You'll be glad you did."

—ANNA BROWN, WIFE OF STEVE BROWN, KEY LIFE MINISTRIES, ORLANDO, FLORIDA

"Knowing Becky Hunter as a truly devout Christian woman and a devoted wife, I am sure the Lord truly blessed her with divine inspiration in writing this book. I pray all who read it will be especially blessed."

—EUDORA CAMPESE, WIFE OF THE RIGHT REVEREND LOUIS CAMPESE, BISHOP TO THE EASTERN SEABOARD OF THE ANGLICAN CHURCH, ORLANDO, FLORIDA

"No matter what your age, you should read this book before and then again after your wedding day and learn how to unwrap the unique power that God intends for marriage. I have known Becky since 1985—as our pastor's wife, our daughter's biology teacher, and as a friend. I can tell you that her love for Christ is obvious in her relationship with her husband, sons, church, and community. Becky's marriage radically reflects the joy that results when you choose *Being Good to Your Husband on Purpose*."

—BEVERLY DAYTON, AUTHOR OF CROWN MINISTRIES' CHILDREN'S BOOKS AND WIFE OF HOWARD DAYTON, CEO OF CROWN FINANCIAL MINISTRIES, GAINESVILLE, GEORGIA

"Becky Hunter has done a masterful job of expressing God's heart on marriage…through a beautiful word picture: God presents a wife as a precious, unique gift to her husband. She deftly navigates the dangerous waters of unfulfilled expectations, however, by drawing our attention away from a focus on how we would desire to be treasured as a gift by our husbands to setting our hearts completely on pleasing the Lord, the One who made us such a valuable gift."

—JUDY DOUGLASS, FOUNDING EDITOR OF CAMPUS CRUSADE FOR CHRIST'S AWARD-WINNING MAGAZINE, *WORLDWIDE CHALLENGE*, AUTHOR OF THREE BOOKS AND WIFE OF STEVEN DOUGLASS, PRESIDENT OF CAMPUS CRUSADE FOR CHRIST INTERNATIONAL, ORLANDO, FLORIDA

"With humor, encouragement, wisdom, and practicality, Becky Hunter has written a book that should be read by every Christian woman who desires a better marriage. Get the tools you need to build a marriage that lasts—the principles in this book work! Don't miss it!"

—CAROL KENT, FOUNDER AND PRESIDENT OF "SPEAK UP"
SPEAKER SERVICES, AUTHOR OF SIX BOOKS, INCLUDING
BECOMING A WOMEN OF INFLUENCE AND WIFE OF GENE KENT,
PORT HURON, MICHIGAN

"Becky knows how to tell it like it is with candor and humor while gently exposing the deadly root causes of failure to be the wife our husband needs. This book should be on the nightstand of every wife and read several times until we can live out the principles to our own surprise and our husband's delight. Learning to be a 'present to your husband from the Lord' may be the best present you give yourself!"

—RITA PETERSON, WIFE OF ROY PETERSON,
PRESIDENT OF WYCLIFFE BIBLE TRANSLATORS,
ORLANDO, FLORIDA

"Becky's bold statement, 'Only a woman of strength can submit,' rings true. This courageous book paints a refreshing picture of marriage as a partnership, not a battleground. If you have any interest in strengthening and enhancing your marriage, this book is for you."

—DEANNA WIEBE, PHARMACEUTICAL RESEARCH TECHNICIAN AND WIFE OF
SCOTT WIEBE, MANAGER OF THE BILLY GRAHAM EVANGELISTIC ASSOCIATION OF CANADA,
WINNIPEG, MANITOBA

Being Good
to Your Husband on Purpose

Becky Hunter

CREATION
HOUSE
PRESS

BEING GOOD TO YOUR HUSBAND ON PURPOSE by Becky Hunter
Published by Creation House Press
A part of Strang Communications Company
600 Rinehart Road
Lake Mary, FL 32746
www.creationhouse.com

Unless otherwise noted, all Scripture quotations are from the Holy Bible, New International Version. Copyright © 1973, 1978, 1984, International Bible Society. Used by permission.

Scripture quotations marked KJV are from the King James Version of the Bible.

Scripture quotations marked NAS are from the New American Standard Bible 2000. Copyright 1960, 1962, 1963, 1968, 1971, 1972, 1973, 1975, 1977 by the Lockman Foundation. Used by permission.

Cartoons by Chip Coburn
Contact information for Chip Coburn: napkinart@aol.com

Cover photograph by J. D. Hunter
Cover design by Rachel Campbell, Strang Communications

Library of Congress Catalog Card Number: 2001090385
International Standard Book Number: 0-88419-789-1

01 02 03 04 05   7 6 5 4 3 2 1
Printed in the United States of America

Dedication

*I dedicate this book to my husband,
Joel Carl Hunter. One lifetime is not
enough to spend with him. I am so grateful
that throughout eternity we will share
in our greatest joy—to praise
and worship God.*

Acknowledgments

I am so grateful to God for the privilege of writing this book and for other blessings too numerous to count; and for the incredible encouragement and insights of my husband, Joel, and our family, Joshua and Lisa, Isaac and Rhonda, and Joel.

My heartfelt appreciation to Vonette Bright for writing the foreword. She has always been an inspiration to me as she has partnered with her husband to point millions of people toward a personal relationship with Jesus Christ.

Particular thanks to Alan Bell, Ron and Kim Hauser, Kelly Hauser, Isaac Hunter, Lisa Hunter, and Rebecca Ramsay for donating many hours to preliminary editing.

Thank you to the following people for their insights, encouragements, and critiques of the manuscript: Brigitt Berry, Steve Bruton, Sandy Covert, Dana Dionne, Lori Droppers, Liz Gritter, Cindy Hobart, Jennifer Johnson, Doris Laser, Roxane Mann, Stacy Miller, Bonnie Mitchell, Nancy Niemetschek, Dawn Norat, Lynda Pederson, Connie Rainwater, Suz Remus, Bob and Bev Towles, and Ann West.

Thanks to Peggy Riley for praying with me and to Jill Howell for her above-and-beyond help and cheerful encouragement.

Special thanks to Philip Crosby, who came up with the perfect title for this manuscript, and to Chip Coburn for the wonderful cartoons.

My sincere gratitude goes to my editor at Creation House Press, Deborah Poulalion, for her editorial expertise and professionalism; to Allen Quain for walking me through the process; to Rachel Campbell for the cover design; to Karen Stott for the layout; to Carolyn Smith for copyediting and to Stephen Strang and Dave Welday for publishing this book.

And last, but not least, an extra special thanks to Dianne DeVoe Walker, my lifelong friend, who first introduced me to Joel, the husband I enjoy being good to on purpose.

Contents

Foreword

This book is an easy read and full of practical suggestions for the woman who has had little mentoring and few examples of what it means to follow the biblical perspective of being a helper to your husband. Becky is a great model for *Being Good to Your Husband on Purpose,* as she has had years of experience and biblical knowledge.

The secular worldview and the biblical worldview are at odds in our culture today probably more than at any time since our nation's founding. One of the areas in which the difference is most evident is in the husband-and-wife relationship.

God gave His textbook to mankind to direct us in how to relate to Him, to each other, to husbands, wives, parents, and children. The timeless principles of the Bible are the greatest guide anyone can follow for life, and certainly for marriage.

Today, little biblical instruction is given to either husband or wife in how to fulfill each of their roles. Tragically, the joyful marriage, the happy home, and the security of children are suffering as a result. One of the greatest areas of conflict is over the misunderstood concept of submission. Becky Hunter writes well to this subject.

After 53 years of marriage to Bill, after trial and error (I have made lots of mistakes), and after having spoken for years to women on the subject of marriage, I have recently come across two words that make the connection more clear between "submission" and "love" in marriage. The two words are "voluntary" and "sacrificial." The wife's submission to her husband is "voluntary" and the husband's love to his wife is "sacrificial"—just as we "voluntarily" submit to Christ, and Christ "sacrificially" loved and died for the church. Dear ones, it works! And you can have fun and fulfillment as you are a helper to your husband and are seriously and playfully *Being Good to Your Husband on Purpose.* Becky has given creative, good, sound advice. Read it! Use it! Enjoy it!

—VONETTE BRIGHT
CO-FOUNDER, ALONG WITH HER HUSBAND,
DR. BILL BRIGHT, OF CAMPUS CRUSADE FOR CHRIST INTERNATIONAL

Introduction

*Marriage teaches you loyalty, forbearance
self-restraint and a lot of other qualities you wouldn't
need so badly if you'd stayed single.*[1]

—*Jimmy Townsend*

I had been married less than a year when I overheard a
woman I admire say, "According to Scripture, a wife is
a gift to her husband from the Lord." The idea of God
looking around for a present to give Joel, and then choosing
me, put an image in my mind that still impacts my life
every day. That thought has always made me want to be my
best not only for Joel, but also for God.

You, too, are a gift from the Lord to your husband.
Through this book, I hope to inspire you to unwrap the
unique power that God intends for your marriage. I want to
encourage you to be good to your husband on purpose—for
your sake, for your husband's sake, and for God's sake.
Consider these words of wisdom:

> He who finds a wife finds what is good and receives
> favor from the LORD.
>
> —PROVERBS 18:22

1

> Houses and wealth are inherited from parents, but a prudent wife is from the LORD.
>
> —PROVERBS 19:14

God said *you* can be a good and prudent wife, and you don't have to do it alone. The greatest confidence-giver and encouragement-builder of all time is with you:

> For I am convinced that neither death nor life, neither angels nor demons, neither the present nor the future, nor any powers, neither height nor depth, nor anything else in all creation, will be able to separate us from the love of God that is in Christ Jesus our LORD.
>
> —ROMANS 8:38–39

Scripture is clear about what it takes to be a present, or gift, to your husband. It takes being a respectful helper and companion whose relationship is both unique and specific to him.

If the idea of being a respectful helper ticks you off, I'm not surprised.

It is interesting that God's solution to man being alone was to bring him a helper. This indicates that from God's perspective you are a helper to your husband if you are committed to him and to your relationship. When your husband can count on you, he is not alone.

> The LORD God said, "It is not good for the man to be alone. I will make a helper *suitable for him.*"
>
> —GENESIS 2:18, EMPHASIS ADDED

However, each one of you also must love his wife as

he loves himself, *and the wife must respect her husband.*

—EPHESIANS 5:33, EMPHASIS ADDED

I WILL BECAUSE GOD WILLS

How sad it is that marriages these days seem to fall apart more easily than newspapers in the rain. As divorce rates escalate, you would think that God's advice on spousal relationships would be vigorously sought out. Regrettably, that is not the case.

Many feminists continue to seek a break from traditional marital roles. Their cries for more power, more freedom, and more options come from every media source imaginable. And, honestly, such thoughts seem attractive in some ways. But like mirages in the desert, they are empty promises, words without results, and claims without truth. God's way is always best—so Scripture is the place to find out how to have authentic power, freedom, and options.

> *"I will because God wills" is the basis of interaction with your husband— not "I will if he will."*

If the idea of being a respectful helper ticks you off, I'm not surprised. Nothing about the way most of us were raised, formally educated, encouraged by friends, or instructed by the media would indicate that the words *respectful helper* should be used to define a wife.

If your mental image of a respectful, helpful wife does not come from Scripture, then you are left with an irritating misconception—that submission looks the same in every relationship. The woman turns into a doormat. Nothing could be further from the truth.

God created you to be a woman of strength and passion. If you live like a wimp, you have definitely missed the point. Accepting the role of wife with a spirit of resignation won't work either, and it is not fun. On the other hand, purposing to be good to your husband—giving him the very best you have to offer—opens your life to incredible continual input from God.

"I will because God wills" is the basis of interaction with your husband—not "I will if he will." In other words, purpose to live and love for God and experience wife-life without regret. Purposing to be good to your husband doesn't stifle you—it frees you; it doesn't degrade you—it lifts you up; it doesn't require obedience—it requires choosing to serve Christ in a simple, challenging way. Christ is the One who can give you both a desire to be your best and the strength to make the effort.

> The wise woman builds her house, but with her own
> hands the foolish one tears hers down.
>
> —Proverbs 14:1

To become a wise builder, learn what God's Word has to say about life and relationships. God's truth is consistent. Know what God said so that you can evaluate all additional input. The arts, sciences, technologies, and even entertainment have the potential to help you get a more godly perspective. On the other hand, each of these areas can offer you quite the opposite. Selective input requires effort, but it's worth it. Maybe the latest research on the differences between men and women could give you ideas on better ways to communicate with your husband. Perhaps watching a comedy spoof about today's family would draw your attention to something that you were unaware of in your own family life. Use God's truth to filter, not fear, all that you see and hear. You will be amazed by the many things God will use to strengthen your household.

The fabulous person you want to be and the great marriage

you want to have require you to have a godly perspective and to live a disciplined life. Look at all of life—especially *your* relationship with *your* husband—from a perspective that includes, but is not limited to, your own.

To be a helper (complement) you have to come to understand *your* husband's perspective, interests, motivation, etc. One way to do this is to study him in the same way you did before you were married. Take the time *to again look at* him. In other words, respect him. Respect literally means "to again look at." Once you understand his perspective, what you give, what you do, and what you say can all become gifts to him. No one else is in the position you are to give your husband what he needs to feel respected, supported, and befriended in your marriage.

When you truly respect your husband and consider how to be the best helper you can be in your life together, there is no pressure to compare your efforts to be a wonderful wife to those of anyone else. Neither is there pressure for you to have the best husband. In fact, if that is your real goal, you will meet with great frustration. As a wife who is a gift, you have only the challenge of faithfully keeping the perspective God has given you and acting consistently on that as He leads you.

Marriage is at its best when both parties offer all they can. However, if one person gives more than the other, that still builds into the relationship. So if your husband does not respond in a way that encourages you, don't quit being your best self. Keep trying, since regret is seldom the result of effort but the lack thereof. God gave you your role as a wife, and it is an honorable one. Whether or not your husband correctly fulfills his role, you can still respond to God. You can offer your best, and doing so will honor both God and your husband. Also, you will have the incredible confidence that comes from knowing that you are doing all God has presented for you to do to make your marriage the best it can be.

...Press on to take hold of that for which Christ Jesus
took hold of [you].

—PHILIPPIANS 3:12

PURPOSING TO BE PERFECT

Unfortunately, neither you nor I will ever be perfect in this
life, but there is great merit and a renewing energy in
purposing toward that goal. In Greek, the language in which
the New Testament was written, *teleos* (translated *perfect*)
actually means "to be fitted for the task." For example, the
screwdriver is the perfect tool for placing a screw in the wall,
but it would be quite inadequate for pounding in a nail.
Likewise, when you strive for perfection as a wife, it is
specific to the partnership between you and your husband.

When used as a verb, *perfect* means "to improve." It is
that action word that inherently challenges us to persevere.
Once you adopt that desire and make it your own, the only
possible failure is giving up on yourself. Don't give up!
God is on your side.

> ...Make every effort to add to your faith goodness;
> and to goodness, knowledge; and to knowledge,
> self-control; and to self-control, perseverance; and
> to perseverance, godliness; and to godliness,
> brotherly kindness; and to brotherly kindness, love.
> For if you possess these qualities in increasing
> measure, they will keep you from being ineffective
> and unproductive in your knowledge of our LORD
> Jesus Christ.
>
> —2 PETER 1:5–8

Chapter One

Encouragement

Strategic Support

Flatter me, and I may not believe you. Criticize me, and I may not like you. Ignore me, and I may not forgive you. Encourage me, and I will not forget you.[1]
—William Arthur Ward

In the movie *The Poseidon Adventure,* the ocean liner SS *Poseidon* is on the open sea when it runs into an enormous storm. A deluge of water crashes through the ballroom. Men in tuxedos and women in evening gowns scream and run. Lights go out, smoke pours into rooms, and, because of the air trapped inside the body of the ship, the ocean liner overturns and floats upside down.

In the confusion the passengers can't figure out what has happened. They scramble to get out—most by dragging themselves along the steps to the top deck. The problem is, the top deck is now one hundred feet under water. Those who try to reach the top of the ship drown.

The survivors are those who do what doesn't make sense. They do the opposite of what everyone else is doing and go into the dark belly of the ship until they reach the hull. By going toward the bottom of the ship, they reach the ocean's surface. Outside, rescuers hear them banging on the hull and cut them free.

In marriage, it's as if God has turned the ship over. The only way to find freedom is to choose what doesn't make sense: lay down your life by serving, supporting, and encouraging the one you married.[2] The truth is that when you "lower" yourself to meet these challenges, you don't find darkness and despair; instead you find a breath of fresh air—both personally and in your marriage.

The strategic disposition required to become an encouraging and supportive wife is the opposite of the one that focuses on not letting your husband get "overly confident." So, if you think your job is to keep your husband from getting the big head and to "bring him down a notch or two," you are thinking upside down.

I can't tell you how many times I have heard a woman say, "At work people think he is just the greatest, and when he gets home I have to bring him back to reality." If a husband were to speak like this to his wife, it would be considered verbal abuse.

What is the intention of a wife who does this? Why does she feel as if she has to convince the man she married he is not the greatest? The answers to that question range from personal insecurities to a weird sense of humor. Ruth Graham profoundly addressed this issue with her comment, "It is God's job to keep him humble; it is my job to love him."[3]

> ## *No one should be able to outdo you in encouraging your husband.*

There are probably several reasons, including some of the following, as to why your husband feels so good about himself at work. In that environment, people admire him and treat him with respect. They follow up on the details of his projects so that he can look his best to outsiders. They take the time to shower, comb their hair, and dress in something attractive. And, perhaps most encouraging of all to him, there are people there who smile. But none of them are doing anything you can't do better. If you put into practice some of the suggestions presented in this book, it won't be long before people at his work may wonder why your husband feels so good about himself at home.

Have you ever noticed how many women shape up emotionally and physically following a divorce? They do so for a man they *hope* to meet. If they can do that under those horrendously difficult circumstances, it must be possible for anyone.

Can you think of a better gift to give your husband than *you* at your best? Your efforts toward improvement may even encourage him as much as the actual achievement of your goal. Making good choices every day virtually guarantees positive results in your attitude and your appearance. There are no big surprises in the ways to accomplish that—spend time with God, eat right, exercise, and get enough rest. It would surely be great if doing those things were as easy as saying them! Efforts to better yourself will be worth it, though.

Practically every married man I know would like nothing better than a truly content, loving, and fairly attractive wife. You can encourage your husband and strengthen your relationship by being your best self.

Neither your mood nor your busy schedule should prevent you from consistently giving your husband positive input. Every day take the time to tell him something you admire about him. Tell him often that you think it is a privilege to be married to him. Tell him how grateful you are for specific things he has done. And, most importantly, tell him you are always praying for God's blessings to fill his life, and then do it. No one should be able to outdo *you* in encouraging *your* husband.

9

Now and then, Jill goes a little overboard
to let Jim know he is important.

Therefore encourage one another and build each other up…

—1 Thessalonians 5:11

(en)COURAGE HIM!

Never underestimate anyone's insecurities. Every person has them, including your husband. When you tell your husband what you admire about him, what you respect about his character, how proud you are of his achievements, or anything for which you are grateful to him, you are putting courage into him. When you say wonderful things about him to other people and he finds out or overhears you, you have encouraged him in yet another significant way.

If you aren't the president of your husband's fan club, campaign for the office. To encourage literally means "to give courage to," and when you dare to shower your husband with sincere praise, you build up his confidence. When you respect him, it is a very significant encouragement to him. Scripture invites you to choose to encourage him in this way. "…Let the wife see that she respects her husband" (Ephesians 5:33, NASB).

Another profound way to "give him courage" is to pray and to ask God to encourage him. God knows exactly what will hearten your husband and has all the means available to provide the perfect inspiration for him. So, as you go through your day, every time you are reminded of him, pray for him.

A good way to practice this discipline is to see the stuff that irritates you as prayer reminders, instead of annoyances. These things include (but are not limited to):

- his half-finished project that *must not* be moved from the dining room table

- the empty cereal boxes neatly closed and placed back on a shelf, or full ones left open on the counter

- his dirty laundry that never makes it to the clothes hamper

Rather than trying to figure out how to get him to change his ways, use these "attention grabbers" to jump-start your prayers for him. In other words, try hitting your knees instead of battering your husband. Prayer is a much more productive use of your time.

It won't be long before you see every trace of your husband—whether annoying or pleasing—as a reminder to invite God to do something wonderful for him. Pray that God will encourage him throughout the day and that he will have the energy for his work. Pray that he will have the proper attitude to be good to his co-workers. Pray for him to have wisdom when he has to deal with unexpected situations. Pray for a break in his busy schedule that will refresh him. Your husband will be blessed.

Additional results of prayers like these include reduced irritation about your husband's quirks and increased personal spiritual maturity. Your ability to offer encouragement improves with spiritual growth. The God-given confidence that comes with being spiritually mature will allow you to elevate someone else.

TIMING IS EVERYTHING

One night not long after Joel and I were married, I was suddenly awakened by music. In my drowsiness, I fumbled with the alarm clock to no avail. That was because it wasn't the alarm. It was a full-volume rendition of *Amazing Grace* resounding from the church chimes across the street. Joel, who was serving as the minister of the church, immediately recognized the pastoral challenge of the moment. He leaped from our bed, and sprinted across the street to the church. He managed to unlock the main door and then raced down a dark hallway into the furnace room. In the dark he found the circuit breakers and flipped the switch for the chimes. Mmmmmmp...*Amazing Grace* ended in a drone. The music was awesome, but at 3:00 A.M. the timing could not have been worse.

Timing is an important aspect of life in general and is even a part of encouragement. If you make your husband's favorite dessert the day he starts his new diet, your heart may be right, but your timing is wrong. If you throw a surprise party in his honor after he has worked a fourteen-hour shift, no matter how great your intentions, the chance he will feel encouraged by your actions is slim.

A good way to time encouragement well is to do things that he will discover naturally as he moves through his day. The possibilities are endless: be ready to walk out the door fifteen minutes before it's time to leave together; place his socks in matched pairs in the drawer; buy his family birthday cards and let him sign them; place encouraging notes in his suitcase; clean his car and fill the tank with gas; take out the trash, even if it is *his* job. You know him; you know what will most encourage him.

If you are at a loss as to how or what to do to encourage your husband, there is a simple method you can use to help you with ideas. Think of things that you would like your daughter-in-law to say and do for your son. Or, consider how you would like your sister-in-law to treat your brother. Or, think about ways you would like to see your mother care for your father. That can help you be more creative in your own marriage.

NO THANKS

Your encouragement has an even greater impact when you do not need to get credit for your efforts. God notices your efforts, whether your husband does or not, and He is pleased by your choice to make a difference. Don't take issue with your husband if he fails to appreciate your efforts. Too often encouragement is lost because a thank-you is missing. If this is something that causes you to struggle, flip a switch in your thinking and—once you get past the drone of your dying egotism—you can have the amazing grace to be content with little or no response from your husband.

> *Offering encouragement when he needs it, even if that is when you least feel like giving it, is really important.*

If you require recognition for your efforts, you may end up timing your efforts to encourage him based on *your* need for appreciation. This doesn't do much for the relationship because your extra-mile efforts for him will lead him to assume that you want something. Offering encouragement when *he* needs it, even if that is when you least feel like giving it, is really important.

It's wonderful if your husband notices your efforts and says thanks, but here's the reason it's not critical: When you encourage him, you are not looking for a specific response; you are investing in the relationship for the long term.

ENCOURAGEMENT THROUGH IT ALL

The influential psychologist Carl Rogers made this comment about trying to change people:

> When I walk on the beach to watch the sunset I do not call out, "A little more orange over to the right, please," or "Would you mind giving us less purple in the back?" No, I enjoy the always-different sunsets as they are. We do well to do the same with people we love.[4]

Before you state your opinions, make your comments, or offer constructive criticism, consider how your words will sound to your husband. You may have a temptation to point out his shortcomings—a.k.a., differences from the way you would do something. However, there is much to be said for looking at the big picture and letting go of the little things that temporarily annoy you but will not make much of a difference in the long run. Pray about your input into his life, and always make that input as encouraging as you possibly can.

One of my favorite verses is Philippians 4:8: "Whatever is true, whatever is noble, whatever is right, whatever is pure, whatever is lovely, whatever is admirable—if anything is excellent or praiseworthy—think about such things." Look for those things in your husband, and your countenance alone will be an encouragement to him.

IN-LAW SUPPORT

While you are thinking about excellent and praiseworthy things, let me ask you to consider the following question: How do you feel about your in-laws? They did raise the man you married, but that alone may not give you the motivation you need to be good to your in-laws on purpose. However, there is an excellent reason to make that choice. When you hold his parents in high regard, you encourage his commitment to family. You reinforce the primacy of those relationships, and ultimately that benefits your nuclear family.

A loving attitude toward his mom and dad will keep you from holding a grudge and stop you from griping to your husband about them. If your husband knows you care about his parents, his life is going to be an easier one. There are positive ways that you can build the relationship with his family, and in the process actually improve your attitude toward them. Here are a few examples beyond the standard ones of sending birthday and Christmas cards or presents:

- Send your mother-in-law flowers on your husband's birthday and thank her for raising your wonderful husband.

- Call or write his parents and tell them you and your husband were thinking of them.

- Overlook any residual parenting they do when they are with your husband and let your awareness of their irritating habits (like rearranging your furnishings or telling you how you could be a better wife or mother) be your instruction guide to someday become the mother-in-law you always wanted.

TIME WITH THE GUYS

Maybe your in-laws are not the ones causing you distress, but instead your challenge is your husband's friends. If your husband seems to require lots of "guy time," you have an additional way to offer encouragement and support. You can react graciously to his friends. Sometimes that interaction is directly with them. More often, though, it simply requires that you are willing to let your husband enjoy his time with them. The time your husband spends with the guys may frustrate you. You may even wonder how the same man who had the good sense to choose you for a spouse could be so foolish as to befriend these people.

If your husband has friends who drag him down, make certain your comments to him concerning the situation focus only on improving the circumstances. Say, for example, your spouse drinks heavily when he is with his friends, or he gets into conversations that you feel could tempt him away from you. Those are certainly valid subjects for discussion.

Limit your expressions of concern to the behaviors that result from the relationships. Do not criticize his friends. If you do, your husband may be the first to remind you that Scripture says, "Do not judge…" (Matthew 7:1). In that passage, to judge means to condemn. Condemning a person and evaluating his actions are not the same. In fact, there is a strong implication in Galatians that a Christian can be a "fruit inspector."

All I said was "Have a good weekend with your friends,"...and he fainted!

> But the fruit of the Spirit is love, joy, peace, patience, kindness, goodness, faithfulness, gentleness and self-control...
>
> —GALATIANS 5:22–23

If the qualities you see growing out of his relationships are essentially the opposites of those listed as fruit of the Spirit, then out of your love for your spouse, calmly express your concerns. He may be willing to listen to what you have to say about situations and behaviors, but the minute you jab at his friends, emotions will rule. Reason always offers the possibility of reaching a goal, but emotions often cloud the way to it.

If your husband has a choice between spending time with good-ole'-so-and-so or an angry, pouting wife, his struggle to choose will be brief. Your demeanor, like a magnet, has dual potential—it can draw your husband to you or repel him.

DEPART FROM YOUR PARENTS AND ARRIVE IN YOUR HUSBAND'S HEART

There is only one statement about marriage that God includes four times in the Bible. Genesis 2:24, Matthew 19:5, Mark 10:7–8 and Ephesians 5:31 all indicate that a good marital relationship necessitates leaving your father and mother, and cleaving to your spouse. Leaving and cleaving are God's request of you, and they are ways to encourage your husband.

Choosing to be a good partner means that your relationship to your parents needs to be radically different than it was when you were single. Once you are someone's wife, you are not your parents' little girl. A new and great relationship can begin with your parents once you have married. However, there is a very good chance that *you* will have to initiate that new and great relationship.

Here are some basic principles that will help you make the transition from their daughter to his partner. Do not depend on your parents for affection, approval, assistance, or counsel. Never give your husband the impression that he is contending with your parents to see if he can fulfill your desires as well or better than they can. That will do nothing but discourage him. When you are more concerned about your husband's ideas, opinions, and practices than those of your parents, you offer him tremendous encouragement.

Leaving your parents isn't really a matter of geography; it is a matter of the heart. It is possible to leave your father and mother and still live next door; but, conversely, it is possible to live a thousand miles away and not leave them. If your parents are honoring God with their lives, then your choice to leave them and prioritize your commitment to your husband and marriage will eventually encourage them, too.

On the other hand, if you had a lousy relationship with your parents when you were growing up and you are relieved to be away from them, now is the time to eliminate any bad attitudes toward them. If you don't, you can be tied emotionally to them in a way that doesn't allow you to leave them. When your attitudes and actions spring from animosity toward, fear of, or frustration with your parents, you haven't left. The wise counsel Romans 12:18 offers is, "If it is possible, as far as it depends on you, live at peace with everyone."

Honor your parents by praying for them, forgiving them (again and again if necessary), and by making your husband-and-wife relationship your priority human relationship. When you get your heart right concerning your parents, your life with your husband benefits.

> Honor your father and your mother, as the LORD your God has commanded you, so that you may live long and that it may go well with you in the land the LORD your God is giving you.
> —DEUTERONOMY 5:16

After you leave, cleave. God's kind of marriage involves

a total commitment of a man and a woman to each other, so choose to cleave through sickness and health, poverty and wealth, pleasure and pain, joy and sorrow, good times and bad times, agreements and disagreements. Your husband will be filled with courage when he knows you are a cleaver—committed to him for life.

LET HIM ENCOURAGE YOU

If your husband is trying to encourage you, receive it. For many women, it is even more difficult to accept support than it is to offer it. You may have been taught from childhood to brush off support with excuses or to water down compliments with suspicion. If your husband is tossing a compliment in your direction, make the attempt to catch it, even if you have to move out of your comfort zone to do so. If he gives you a compliment, simply say thank you. Don't make him spend time convincing you he really meant it. If you do, he is likely to withhold his future compliments until he has an hour to back them up.

Always try to find
the best in every word he says
and every action he takes.

Learn how to receive the positives in his comments, even if they are only implied. There is no benefit in minimizing his potentially encouraging words by filtering them through slight paranoia. Train yourself to hear encouragement in what your husband says. For instance, if he crawls into bed and says, "I love clean sheets," you may think:

- He must think I don't wash the sheets often enough.

- Does he think those sheets clean themselves? I

don't think it ever occurs to him that I work very hard around here.

• Oh great! I'm in a negligee and he notices the sheets.

Instead, hear what he has implied by his comment: "I love how you take care of the details to make my life this pleasant." Instead of requiring him to say that, *require yourself to hear that.* Always try to find the best in every word he says and every action he takes.

ROSE-COLORED GLASSES AND MORE

Joel and I were having coffee one evening with a young, newly engaged couple. The soon-to-be bride was effervescent as she described their romantic engagement and wedding plans. Then she looked quite serious and said, "I'm going to enjoy every moment now, because I know that soon I will have to take off the rose-colored glasses."

"Why?" I asked.

"Oh, I know when we are actually married and are dealing with the hassles of everyday life, that I will need to be realistic."

"Leave them on," I said. "You will still see reality, and it will look its best."

The purpose of any lens is to use the light passing through it to form a clearly visible image. Because I am a Christian, the lenses I choose to look through—or, to put it another way, my rose-colored glasses—are the personal relationship I have with Jesus Christ. When I look at my husband, I see him clearly through my relationship with Jesus, so I can see him as Christ sees him.

That lens allows me to see his motives, his dreams, his enthusiasm, his cares, and his joys greatly magnified. Through that same lens, I see his faults significantly minimized. In fact, sins for which he has asked forgiveness from God are not even in my realm of vision. As a result, I am in touch with the reality that matters.

Offering encouragement and accepting it when it is given to you is easier if you look at your husband through the best-perspective lenses. God loves your husband so much, and He would love to help you focus on why He does. Ask Him for a pair of rose-colored glasses to replace the ones you lost.

CHAPTER ONE:
ENCOURAGEMENT

❧

1. List three ways you could encourage your husband.

   _____

   _____

   _____

2. Give some examples of helpful encouragement and some examples of encouragement that might be counter-productive.

   _____

   _____

   _____

   _____

   _____

   _____

   _____

3. What requests can you be lifting to the Lord on behalf of your husband "to give him courage"?

   _____

   _____

   _____

   _____

   _____

   _____

4. List some characteristics of your marriage and of your husband that are:

- true _____

  _____

- noble _____

  _____

- right _____

  _____

- pure _____

  _____

- lovely _____

  _____

- admirable _____

  _____

- excellent _____

  _____

- praiseworthy _____

  _____

and "think about such things" (Philippians 4:8).

5. What are some things that your husband does to attempt to encourage you? How can you be more receptive to his efforts?

_____

_____

_____

_____

_____

_____

_____

CHAPTER ONE:
ENCOURAGEMENT

ͽ⸙ͼ

MAKING IT PRACTICAL

- Pray for your husband *and* encourage him a minimum of twice a day, every day (in a way that is significant to him).

- Receive any and every effort your husband makes to give you encouragement with a sincere thank-you. (No rebuttals or denials allowed.)

- Write a letter to your in-laws and thank them for sacrificing and investing in the life of their son. Tell them how much you love your husband, their son. Write your parents and thank them for raising you. Include positive comments about your husband in their letter, as well.

Chapter Two

Submission Impossible?

Role and Reason

*Marriage is like twirling a baton, turning
handsprings or eating with chopsticks.
It looks easy until you try it.*[1]
—Helen Rowland

After one month of marriage, Lori determined that picking up Karl's crumpled jeans on their bedroom floor was not her job. She wanted to make sure that any thoughts her wonderful, new husband might have about her being his maid were nipped in the bud. After three days of jeans lying on the floor, Lori was mad. While it was not bothering her husband that his jeans were lying on the floor in the middle of their bedroom, she could think of almost nothing else. She waited until Karl arrived home from work that evening and then she stomped into the bedroom and, with a melodramatic sigh, reached over and scooped up the jeans. As she did, she noticed something—they were *her* jeans. Nearly twenty years later, Lori says her marriage benefited greatly from that one incident.

Lori, like many of us, was apprehensive that her role as a wife could, in some way, limit her personal potential and conceivably minimize all she had to offer. So, on high alert for signals indicating that might be the case, she began watching for slights from the man she loved rather than looking for ways to support and encourage him.

> *In reality, a submissive spirit*
> *is an awesome gift specifically for you to give*
> *your husband; but, like many others,*
> *you may believe that gift is a curse.*

Because we have been inundated with reports of misuse and abuse, the power of submission has been lost to the headlines. In reality, a submissive spirit is an awesome gift *specifically for you to give your husband;* but, like many others, you may believe that gift is a curse. That is due both to a misunderstanding of Scripture and to a culture that finds submission of a woman to a man—even if that man is her husband—high on the list of what is politically incorrect.

There was a curse in the Garden of Eden. It was not that a wife should submit to her husband. The curse was that a wife *would not want to submit*—hence, your misplaced desire. Genesis 3:16 says, "Your desire will be for your husband, and he will rule over you." In the original language, the word *desire* does not indicate passion, but rather a need to conquer.[2] A contentious attitude is the result of the curse. It is godly to desire to submit; a lack of longing to do so indicates the curse remains.

While it may seem as if you are trying to conquer a specific problem or win an argument with your husband, those aspirations can easily shift from topical to personal and become attempts to conquer him. Whenever you address a difficult situation in your relationship, stay focused on

Some problems have been around
for a long time!

resolving the problem and fight any tendencies you may have to malign your husband.

It takes great strength to submit. Submission is an act of will tied to faith. The literal definition of submission is "to undergird (support) his mission." Submission is thinking of yourself less and of him more. Your real battle is against selfishness.

For many women this seems to beg the question: Why shouldn't he support my mission? Good question, wrong perspective. Submission is *other*-focused and *self*-disciplined. Stop trying to figure out what *he* should be doing and think about what you can do to make a difference in your marriage. Consider how you can take your gifts, talents, and dreams and creatively use them as a contributing partner in your relationship. How can you make a wonderful difference to this man, who once-upon-a-time made your heart skip a beat when he looked your way? Ask yourself, "How can I be good to him *on purpose?*"

God's call on your husband's life didn't leave you out. In fact, God has called you and your husband to become one. Therefore, your husband's mission includes you, needs you, and will suffer without you. This means that your life, your gifts, and your passions can be used to accomplish something great in and through your marriage—not in spite of it.

Proverbs 31 tells of the ideal woman. Her priorities are clearly outlined—God, husband, children, family, and then community. Verses 10–12 reflect on her role as a wife:

> A wife of noble character who can find? She is worth far more than rubies. Her husband has full confidence in her and lacks nothing of value. She brings him good, not harm, all the days of her life.

Her support of her husband did not limit her; it empowered her and blessed him. In the same way, you will find that supporting your husband does not limit you. Your primary ministry is to your husband. The key to that ministry's success is a submissive attitude that makes you his complement, helper, and faithful lover.

For those of you who say, "I will submit only to God." Well, OK, here are His instructions:

> Wives, in the same way be submissive to your husbands so that, if any of them do not believe the word, they may be won over without words by the behavior of their wives, when they see the purity and reverence of your lives.
>
> —1 PETER 3:1–2

> Wives, submit to your husbands, as is fitting in the LORD.
>
> —COLOSSIANS 3:18

> Then they [the older women] can train the younger women to love their husbands and children, to be self-controlled and pure, to be busy at home, to be kind and subject to their husbands, so that no one will malign the word of God.
>
> —TITUS 2:4–5

> Wives, submit to your husbands as to the LORD. For the husband is the head of the wife as Christ is the head of the church, his body, of which he is that Savior. Now as the church submits to Christ, so also wives should submit to their husbands in everything.
>
> —EPHESIANS 5:22

At some point in your life you may find yourself saying, "God, if I just knew what it was You wanted me to do, I would do it." Regarding submission, He has made His desire known and there is nothing complicated about it. Submission is simple—and very difficult. It is difficult because there is no cultural support for it and relatively few godly examples of it. It isn't even mentioned in popular women's magazines; it is criticized in women's studies courses at universities; and it is ridiculed in the TV sitcoms. However, this lack of encouragement should not discourage you from something

God has clearly said is appropriate. There is no need to exhaust yourself trying every other possible option of interaction with your husband before you attempt to do it the way God recommended.

Someone once asked this question of a wife whose long-term marriage was an obvious blessing: "To what do you attribute your successful marriage?"

She replied, "Making good decisions."

"And how did you learn to make good decisions?"

"Making bad decisions."

> *You can resign,*
>
> *surrender, or wimp out on your own;*
>
> *but you can't submit without God.*

Good decisions are godly ones. Save yourself the headache and heartache of trying to be a great wife without a submissive attitude. Choose to honor your husband with a decision to trust God's Word even on this issue.

Submission results from God-given strength and perspective; you cannot be submissive on your own. You can resign, surrender, or wimp out on your own, but you can't submit without God. Because submission is possible only through God's strength and perspective, if your husband ever requests something of you that God has said is sin, you should not submit. That is just common sense because submission is your response to God's request of you, and God does not want you to do anything that He has said He is against.

The purpose of submission to your husband is to honor God—your husband just gets the overflow benefits. You end up blessed too, but your satisfaction is not the reason for being submissive. This concept of overflow benefit reminds me of the young single woman who earnestly

Linda decided to go along with
Matt's vacation idea.

prayed before climbing into bed: "Dear God, I don't ask anything for myself, but I do pray for my mother. Please, give her a handsome son-in-law." No one gets cheated in this paradigm. Everyone wins.

BEING TOGETHER WHEN YOU'RE APART

God made you to be a helper, so it is important to know just what that means. Genesis 2:18 says, "It is not good for the man to be alone. I will make a helper suitable for him." According to the *Wycliffe Bible Commentary,* the colloquial meaning of *helper* is "corresponding one" or "one who talks back."[3] So, if you have ever talked back to your husband, technically you have done something a wife was intended to do from the beginning. No doubt talking to your husband was meant to edify the partnership, but it hasn't always been used for that purpose. When you speak words that *do* build the relationship, Scripture indicates that you help him.

When God put man in the Garden of Eden, God told him to work it and take care of it. (See Genesis 2:15.) Eve was created so that the man wouldn't be alone (v. 18). The man you are married to needs to know he's not alone in his efforts, hopes, or struggles. You may feel as if there is a problem because he desires to spend long hours at the workplace (garden) in which God has placed him, but the real problem occurs when he feels as if he is there without your support.

There are several ways you might be telling your husband that he is alone in his efforts. You may be complaining to your husband, "Why don't you spend more time with me?" instead of saying, "Thanks for all you do to provide for us." Your words imply that unless he is at your side, his efforts do nothing to strengthen your relationship. That simply is not the case; his efforts away from you are, in part, for you.

Being physically near him is not the only way to let him know you support him. Be there for him emotionally (don't let PMS rule the day), try to understand what is important to him, and pray for him. Partner with him in all of these ways to maximize the return on his labor. Almost every man loves accomplishment, so partnering with your husband in these ways has the potential to make a positive difference in your relationship.

MATURITY MATTERS

Your husband needs you to be a faithful, loving, thinking, and mature woman. If your attitude and actions are immature, your husband's life and mission will be affected and the partnership diminished. If you choose to act like a child, then he may feel like he needs to take care of you. If, on the other hand, you act as if you don't need him or choose to declare war on his male ego, then he may focus on protecting himself. Continually give him your best self, and you give him the opportunity to respond to you in kind.

> *Continually give him your best self and you give him the opportunity to respond to you in kind.*

There is no diagram of a perfect marriage. Your marriage is unique. It is not going to be identical to anyone else's. The methods of support you use for *your* husband, might be ones that would actually irritate *my* husband. You are the best one to figure out what you can do to benefit your husband. Maybe he needs you to help by listening, or by being ready to leave "on time." Maybe it really is important to him that your home be a place of hospitality. Maybe you can help by adding to the income, or giving him the guilt-free time and space he needs to accomplish his dream—his mission. Maybe all he really needs from you is a positive attitude—no worrying, whining, or being pushy. The needs are not only different from couple to couple, but also from season to season in the same couple's life.

For example, since Joel and I were married in 1972, I have been—among other things—a high school biology teacher, a stay-at-home mom, a radio ministry administrator, and our church newspaper editor. I was better at some of the adventures than others, but all were based on what I understood at the time to be the most helpful to Joel and to our relationship.

Your husband can't make you submit—no one can. Submission is totally voluntary. It is up to you whether or not you will be submissive in your marriage. You alone get to decide. If you choose to do so, it will better minister to your husband than anything else you could ever do or say. Because it reflects your attitude, it affects every aspect of your lives together. When your heart's desire is to undergird (support) his mission, you will look for every possible way that you can lighten his load.

Your attitude is what matters to God. Submission is not just going along with your husband's decisions because you mindlessly give in. Nor is submission doing what he says while wanting to punch him in the nose. Sitting down on the outside while standing up on the inside will stress you mentally, physically, and spiritually. That doesn't work for the long term—not for you or for your marriage. Instead, you can choose to take steps toward making your *feelings* and *actions* match.

Your emotions may be inconsistent with your actions, but through prayer each can bolster the other. One way to alter your feelings is to change your actions. For example, it has been proven that if you force yourself to smile, you feel happier. Your body chemistry responds to your action. Acting in a loving way toward your husband helps your feelings for him to be more loving. Just understanding the value of being a submissive wife goes a long way in making your desires match your actions, but more important is having faith that God's way is the best way.

AVOID GETTING TRIPPED UP

When my husband asks me to dance, I don't think about how unfair it is for him to lead. I prefer to use my energy to dance. A former governor of Texas, Ann Richards, made a wonderful observation about the way Ginger Rogers danced with Fred Astaire: "She did everything Fred Astaire did. She just did it backwards and in high heels."[4] Joel leads me in the dance because, centuries ago, a respected dance instructor decided the man would lead. So when we dance, I concentrate on following Joel's lead. The dance makes us partners, but it is our acceptance of our preassigned roles—both of which are challenging—that allows us to have a great time and avoid tripping each other.

Marriage is like a dance. Joel was assigned to leadership in our marriage because, centuries ago, God decided the man would lead in that covenant relationship. So in our marriage, I concentrate on following Joel's lead. The marriage makes us partners, but it is our decisions to accept our preassigned roles—both challenging—that allow us to have a great time and avoid tripping each other.

True submission is possible only when you know Jesus Christ. That is because biblical submission is a conscious decision to share the strengths God has given to you with the person He gave you as a partner. Your attitude as you do so is God's gift to you. To support and serve your husband without reservation—with heartfelt enthusiasm—encourages him and strengthens you.

Many wives are tempted to invest part of their energy in diversions that appear to be productive. Putting "all of their eggs in one basket," a.k.a. marriage, seems to be too big a risk. They have a nagging feeling that it is smart to be prepared if "things don't work out," a.k.a. divorce. Contrary to popular opinion, this is not a wise way to live. Your energy should not be wasted on "what ifs." Worst-case scenarios can make you afraid that you are going to turn around someday after ministering to your husband for years and consider yourself an idiot for not putting your own needs first. God certainly wouldn't call that kind of faithfulness idiocy. One of the many assurances we have of His thoughts on this subject is found in 1 Corinthians 10:24: "Nobody should seek [her] own good, but the good of others."

> **A long, healthy, happy marriage is more likely to result from your ministry to your husband than it is from investment in productive diversions.**

The *fear* of giving yourself in ministry to your husband is what can create a distance in your relationship. The truth is, *giving yourself* draws you closer. Jesus made this point: "Where your treasure is, there your heart will be also" (Matthew 6:21). A long, healthy, happy marriage is more likely to result from your ministry to your husband than it is from investment in productive diversions. Since God is the One who gave you the gift of submission and asked you to use it, your practice of it honors Him.

Self-centeredness brings regret, but being God-centered and responding to others accordingly brings joy. You can see the fear of being overridden, taken advantage of, or disregarded in the face of any woman who wears a T-shirt emblazoned with the slogan "The More I Know About Men, the Better I Like My Dog." When the primary focus of submission is the response (reward) from your husband, discouragement will come. *Your giving is for God.* Don't let fear cause you to tell God you aren't interested in His offer to minister to your husband through submission. "There is no fear in love. But perfect love drives out fear..." (1 John 4:18a). It is difficult, if not impossible, to be your best self when you are apprehensive.

WHEN HE JUST WON'T LEAD

Perhaps you are thinking that you would be glad to be a helper to your husband, but he is not about to be the leader in your relationship. Maybe he has stated that, or, more likely, you have simply assumed that from his actions. If your husband has decided marriage is like a game of tag and you're "it," honor him and God by offering your best. When a man rejects the leadership role, the chances are slim that he did so in order to assume the role of helper in the relationship. The bottom line is this: A great vacuum is created by his role rejection. Therefore, make sure the critical spiritual and physical needs of your household are met and let the non-essentials go. You can only do all you can do.

A marriage requires 100 percent from each participant. It is not a 50/50 partnership. In a 50/50 partnership, nothing would be missing if one or the other carried the entire relationship alone by simply upping his or her contribution to 100 percent. But many people know from experience that 100 percent participation from one spouse does not make up for a lack of participation from the other spouse. A marriage works best when both parties give 100 percent. If only one of you gives it your all, there will be gaps. When you feel as if you just pull him along, the journey is really tough. Yet, hand-in-hand, the journey can still be made.

Ask God to reveal to you anything that might be causing your husband to back off from his God-given responsibilities. There may be ways you take away his leadership in some areas without realizing you are doing it, and so he decides that he can coast because you seem to be able to handle everything well. Over time, he may even begin to think you don't need him.

ENCOURAGE HIS LEADERSHIP

Releasing the "reign" in your home is especially difficult when you are confident that you know more than your husband knows about a subject. Even when our three sons were young, Joel sometimes traveled out of town for conferences. After he came home, I would assume that I still had final say on the kids' issues of the past few days. After all, how could he come up with a solution without knowing the week's history? I thought there was no way he knew enough about what was going on in the boys lives, at those moments, to make the best decisions. Everyone knows that kids go to the source that offers the best chance of getting what they want. Naturally, they went straight to Dad with their requests to do this and that.

I told Joel about my concerns, but I also told him that I trusted his decision. Next I did one of the best things I have ever done. I prayed for Joel to make wise decisions; for my attitude to match my expressions; and for our sons to be protected for God's work. When I did that, I was able to relax. I was reminded of what I have always known—God is in control. I don't have to run the universe; He already does a fine job.

I could follow Joel's lead, even when his decision differed from the one I would have made, and God would honor my right actions and attitude. In this specific instance concerning Joel and the boys, I can now see that the situation ultimately helped them to be comfortable turning to their dad even when they weren't so sure of his response but just needed a dad's perspective. And, looking back, there were many times Joel said to the boys, "Go ask your mom. I agree with whatever she says."

When you choose to acknowledge your husband's authority in your marriage, he has no need to try to *prove* he's the leader. Your confidence in him helps him with his God-given role. Deferring to his leadership does not negate your participation in his decision making. Tell him what you would decide if you were in his place and also tell him why you would make that choice. Usually, this is easy to do. Then, after you give him your perspective, tell him you trust his decision. Typically, this is not easy to do. However, with God's help you will be able to do this, too.

Even if you are used to being the main decision-maker, if there is any area of your relationship in which he indicates an interest in leading, let him. When you make that choice you begin to break an imperfect pattern in your marriage. If, instead, you decide to do battle, you risk permanently redefining your roles.

Several years ago I saw a television interview with a discouraged Cambodian woman whose story fascinated me. Through an interpreter, she said that the women in her society are the leaders in their homes and community. That was the way it had been for many years—ever since the men went away to war and the women took on the entire responsibility for their households.

When the men finally came back, the women stayed in their positions instead of welcoming the men back to their traditional leadership roles. Within a few months of their return, most of the men had moved to the outskirts of the village. There, slothfulness and drunkenness had become commonplace. "Can our village ever be like it was before the war?" the Cambodian woman asked with tears in her eyes.

You may be a wife who struggles with very trying circumstances. Your husband may not be away at war, but maybe he travels often with his business, or has very long hours away from the family due to his work. A work shift that makes it necessary for him to sleep while you are awake can make him an almost invisible partner. For all intents and purposes he may be around only on the weekends. To adjust each time to his presence and returning leadership can be an incredible challenge. Choose to meet it. Flex. Encourage his leadership in your home by making it easy for him to suggest ideas, and then go along with his agenda on purpose.

You may have a husband who will lead if you change the way you interact, or you may not. Always pray for the wisdom and strength to be who you need to be in the relationship with your husband. In either scenario, you can have a wife-life with no regrets.

UNLIMITED EXPRESSIONS

When I was eight months pregnant with our first son, my husband and I went to a preparation-for-birthing class. While I hesitate to say it did much to prepare us for that event, I can say we met many interesting people. One who stands out in my mind was Cindy. Cindy also had just a month to go in her pregnancy. Each of the participants seated in the circle "shared." When it was Cindy's turn she said, "I'm Cindy. My baby is due in June. I don't do windows, and I don't do socks."

I thought that was odd. Apparently, I wasn't the only one who thought so, because a lady seated next to her asked the obvious question: "What do you mean, 'you don't do windows and you don't do socks'?"

"When we got married, I told my husband that I would never wash a window and I would never touch his dirty, rolled up, inside-out socks. That set him straight."

Anytime you choose
to emphasize what you won't do, you limit
what could be accomplished. Marriage
thrives on "I dos," not "I don'ts."

Obviously, this was very important to her and several of the women in the room clapped as if to agree. Maybe she was just trying to be funny; but even if she was, the point was sad. Anytime you choose to emphasize what you won't do, you limit what could be accomplished. Marriage thrives on "I dos," not "I don'ts."

Wouldn't you be willing to be at your husband's beck

and call for endless weeks and months to attend to his needs if he were disabled in some way? Then why is it so hard to pick up his socks and praise God that he is blessed with two feet? The big stuff probably is not what will blow you away, but the little stuff may make you go to pieces.

This truth is also evident in nature. Do you realize that all of the hurricanes, monsoons, cyclones, and tornadoes in the world do not destroy as many buildings as termites? It is the accumulation of the little things that has the potential to do extensive damage.

The frequency and repetition of even a minor annoyance by your spouse can tempt you to behave in ways that you would never tolerate from someone else. Don't allow yourself to go there; instead be courteous. Patience is an aspect of a submissive attitude that lets you offer a better response. Beauty and value can result as patience covers the irritant. A pearl is simply a garment of patience that enclosed an annoyance.

> *Respond to your husband*
> *in ways that say, "You are important."*

There are opportunities every day for you to respond positively to your husband:

- He forgot to call you from work.
  "You must have had a really hectic day."

- He forgot your birthday.
  "I'm glad you can overlook my aging."

- He drives miles out of the way because he is lost, but prefers not to stop for directions.
  "Hey, we get to spend more time together—and besides, the scenery is interesting."

Anytime you offer a response, be sure you have first considered your husband's perspective. If he isn't used to you responding in these positive ways, you may need to assure him of your sincerity. Responses like these are ones that you might be likely to use if someone "important" comes into your home. And that is really the point— respond to your husband in ways that say, "You are important." Let each response indicate that you looked for the best in the situation. Never belittle or accuse.

If you struggle with the idea of submission, please keep struggling until you win. Your perseverance is important. There is inevitably a temptation to give up about the time you should gear up.

> Consider it pure joy…whenever you face trials of many kinds, because you know that the testing of your faith develops perseverance. Perseverance must finish its work so that you may be mature and complete, not lacking anything.
>
> —JAMES 1:2–4

GO AHEAD AND SAY IT

You are entitled to your opinions and you can express them. There is no implication in Scripture that there is anything wrong with that. Your ministry to your husband includes saying what you think—not what you think he wants you to say. Say it politely and then muster up all the discipline you have within you and force yourself to drop it. Repetition, tempting as it might be, is ineffective. It can even make it difficult for your husband to want to agree with you. Proverbs 17:1 says, "Better a dry crust with peace and quiet than a house full of feasting, with strife."

For better or worse, a submissive spirit does not tally previous concessions on small matters to use as leverage when it comes to major decisions. In other words, recording the message he wants on the answering machine and handing him the TV remote doesn't mean that you should have final say on whether or not to accept his out-of-state job offer. Figuring he "owes you this time" is calculated manipulation, not submission.

The Bible indicates that your husband carries the burden of final decision making. His decision may be to

- do what you think should be done.

- compromise.

- do it entirely the way he believes God would have him do it.

Your gift is to be able to give him that choice—confidently and consistently, and to know that God is pleased with your part.

CHAPTER TWO:
SUBMISSION IMPOSSIBLE?

MAKING IT PERSONAL

1. What does your husband do well, and how can your support him as he does those things? How would you summarize your husband's mission?

    _____

    _____

    _____

2. What fears do you have in supporting him in his mission?

    _____

    _____

3. What specific ways could you help him without increasing your fears?

    _____

4. In what ways are you tempted to control him and/or the relationship?

    _____

    _____

5. What are some of the potential disadvantages of being a submissive wife? What are some of the advantages?

    _____

    _____

6. Of all the people you know, who do you treat the best? In what ways could you treat your husband to some of those same kindnesses?

    _____

    _____

MAKING IT PRACTICAL

- Ask your husband to tell you what *he* believes to be his specific mission on earth. (Really listen to what he says and ask him how you can help him achieve his goals. Do not try to adjust his mission.)

- Take one investment of your time, energy, money, or whatever else you have deposited somewhere besides your marriage and put it into your marriage. (Here are some examples to get you thinking: quit the women's club and spend that evening with your spouse, or take your secret money and put it into your joint account, or clean his car while he is away on business.)

- Be ready fifteen minutes early for every event you will attend with your husband for the next six months. (After that it will be a habit.)

Chapter Three

Finances

Checkmate

For the love of money is a root of all kinds of evil.
Some people, eager for money, have wandered from the faith
and pierced themselves with many griefs.

—*1 Timothy 6:10*

In the premarital classes offered at our church, a couple of questions always come up during the twelve weeks:

- Do you think it matters if we keep separate bank accounts?

- My fiancé has debt. When we marry, should I help him pay it off?

These questions always amaze me. How can you take his name, give him your heart, give him your body, give him children, but not give him your money? What does that say about the place money has in your life? You either trust this man or you don't, and if you don't, marriage would be a really bad next step. Any woman has the option of not marrying until her fiancé's bills are paid, but refusing to assist with the bill payments after the wedding can block many blessings.

47

Billy and Sue take the "big step"
in marriage!

If you earn money and keep it from your husband, you are withholding a part of yourself from him. Some spouses put funds in a secret account so that they have a backup in case of a marital catastrophe. These "his and hers" accounts drain valuable energy and resources that could be used to compound a husband and wife's interest *in each other.* If you are stashing away funds for reasons that are beneficial to your union, then you won't have to conceal them from your husband. Funds should be put away for your mutual benefit—not so one of you can panic and run. You are in this relationship together for life, and that requires a trust.

FINANCIAL PROBLEMS?

Two people struggling for their dream home may be romantic. Two people in a dream home that leaves them struggling is not. But a wife who chooses to be good to her husband on purpose can minimize the struggle and emphasize the blessings in either situation.

Financial problems? You are not alone. In fact, it is likely that you have either had them, are in the middle of them, or will face them in the future. It is important to learn biblical ways to handle finances. Some excellent resources on this topic are available through Crown Financial Ministries, a national non-denominational Christian work founded by Larry Burkett and Howard Dayton.[1]

However, the challenge of your finances is not the emphasis of this chapter. Instead, it is the challenge of understanding your husband's philosophy of money. Learn to respect him in spite of, or maybe because of, his philosophy. Financial problems in your marriage may seem to result from a lack of money, or from your husband's strange ideas of how the money that you do have should be managed. However, neither a money shortage nor a husband's weird financial strategy can tear apart a relationship. I mean, think about it: somewhere there is a penniless couple living very contentedly in a cabin in the woods—no money, just a husband's out-of-the-way, no-frills, dream house.

> *Two people struggling for their dream home may be romantic. Two people in a dream home that leaves them struggling is not.*

At the same time, somewhere there is a wealthy couple discontentedly living in a mansion—plenty of money and a husband's castle for his family. I use these extremes to make the point that it is possible to be happy with very little, simply because your husband is happy, or to be unhappy with very much in spite of his joy. Most of the time a solution to your financial problems can be found in a change of perspective.

PERSPECTIVE IS EVERYTHING

If you have ever played chess, you know that *checkmate* is the term used to indicate that you are definitely going to win. You will win because there is nowhere the person with whom you were enjoying the game can make a move and continue to play. So, you win—but the game is over, and you realize that playing was the fun part.

If winning *is* more fun than enjoying a relationship with your husband, you are destined for problems. That is because there is no way to celebrate your win without the implied celebration of your partner's loss. In a marriage, finances are often seen as a place where you can win or lose. Whether you see your husband as a cheapskate or a spendthrift, you may think it seems logical to counter his approach in order to balance him out. If you decide to beat the cheapskate by talking him into buying something or to conquer the spendthrift by nagging him into saving, your celebration is likely to be both lonely and brief. Stalemate is not much more fun than checkmate. In stalemate you stop one move short of a win. There is a deadlock—no one wins, no one loses, but there is no more action and no celebration.

When you think about your husband with a God-given perspective, you aren't so interested in winning your point as you are in wanting the relationship to win. I know that nearly every relationship expert in the world praises the art of compromise. And compromise is fine, but it is seldom the cause of a great celebration for either party involved.

> *You will be the happiest when your attitude is one that elevates your husband's happiness to be one of your greatest joys—when you recognize his wins as your wins, too.*

Scripture says that there is joy in giving, in honoring, and in loving. When you are being good to your husband on purpose, you think in terms of what he prefers, not in terms of what he *should* prefer, and certainly not in terms of whether or not it is your turn to get what you want. It's embracing the perspective that you are a gift from the Lord to your husband. You will be the happiest when your attitude is one that elevates your husband's happiness to be one of your greatest joys—when you recognize his wins as your wins, too. You can have that attitude. Pray for it and hope for it more than you hope for a million dollars in the bank. Often, the inexplicable result of your prayers is that God uses the attitude He gives you to bless you in ways you never could even imagine.

THERE IS MUCH TO LOSE

Personal finance may be the most difficult place to keep yourself from putting your husband in checkmate (a position from which he loses if he makes any move). Here are just a few of the ways you can put your husband in checkmate and never even realize you are doing it:

- Continually express (or, from his perspective, nag about) your need to have him work less so that he can be home more and at the same time complain that there isn't enough money.

- Be upset if he spends money on anything that *you* didn't think was needed, even if it was a gift for you.

- Tell your kids that *you* would buy them what they want, but their father says, "We have to learn to save."

Money or the lack thereof does not cause the relationship pain. But holding your husband in checkmate—by giving him the impression that any attempt he makes to better a situation is inappropriate—can cause much misery. Choose to expand your perspective by reviewing his perspective.

PHILOSOPHIES OF FINANCES

Checkbooks are autobiographies. Money is much more than just legal tender or something to exchange for what is desired. In some sense, your husband feels as if the money represents who he is. He traded part of his life to get it, and if he gives it to you he is giving you a part of his life. Spending habits are really statements about him. They say what he values and how he will relate to his environment. Sometimes his trading down in possessions, such as houses or cars, may be trading up in things like priorities or freedom.

Marital disagreements involving money go much deeper than the amount of money you, as a couple, have to spend.

Steve handled the family finances in a way that made perfect sense to him.

There are several different financial philosophies. Consider the philosophies of money management that follow, and choose the one that best reflects your husband's attitude about finances. Then respect your husband by choosing to "again look at" why he spends money where he does. In the process, you can better understand who he is. Here are some commonsense observations about being married to one of five typical financial types—the Saver, the Fun Addict, the Status Seeker, the Artist, and the Aspiring Millionaire.

BEING MARRIED TO THE SAVER

A woman at the bank teller's window was asked to confirm her four-digit code in order to make a withdrawal. "S-A-V-E," she responded and then added, "My husband opened this account and picked that code so every time I withdrew money I would be reminded."

A saver's goals are control and security. There is much power in withholding. It eliminates risks and minimizes vulnerability. At worst, a saver can use power to frustrate your hopes; but, on the other hand, a saver can provide valuable caution and accumulated resources when really needed.

If your husband is a saver, it is likely that he came through a time of scarcity and made the decision that accumulation was the best way to cope with the fear of not having enough for the future. Accumulation means, of course, withholding the goods—in this case, money—so that it can grow in value. A saver thrives on statements like, "A penny saved is a penny earned," and, "Waste not, want not." A saver also usually believes in assumptions like, "A fool and his money are soon parted," and, "Don't trust them any farther than you can throw them." In fact, for a saver, these are words to live by. In a saver's mentality, most people are inclined to try to take *his* hard-earned goods for their own use, and it is likely that his suspicions are based on actual incidents.

So, how do you thrive in a marriage to a saver? Well, if you are also a saver, little negotiation is required. However, if you are naturally inclined to "shop 'til you drop," you may have to recall the way you originally interpreted his attitude about finances. No doubt there was a time when you were actually attracted to the stability of a saver—he seemed to be very mature and have good business sense. You weren't wrong then. You just looked at it differently. Look at it again that way, and the temptations you have to call him cheap may go away.

The worst responses you can offer to a saver are to threaten him—"Loosen up or I'm leaving"—or mock him—"I bought mustard greens for dessert because they were on sale"—or proposition him—"I will make you glad you came to bed tonight if you stop insisting that I return the cashmere sweater." All of these maneuvers, unfortunately, verify in the saver's mind that you are trying to get *his* cache. So his natural reaction is to become even more conservative. If he does give in to your ploys, your victory will do little to move him toward your goal of philanthropy.

A saver may relax a bit if he is totally convinced that you consider him much more important than his goods. Even if the saver doesn't loosen up right away, by showering him with attention, appreciation, and love you can make the wait much more fun.

BEING MARRIED TO THE FUN ADDICT

"If it feels good, do it," is the motto of most kids. If you married your husband because he was a really fun guy and he never changed, you need to respect—look again at—his thinking. A fun addict thinks that the slogan, "Eat, drink, and be merry for tomorrow we die," is the wisest saying in the world. He assumes that he can't do much about the problems of life, so why worry about them? He is not insensitive, but he is not the type to face a problem head on. He avoids problems with humor and, therefore, tends to be popular with people who don't have to live with him. He doesn't mind risk, but he fears boredom.

A fun addict is likely to frustrate you because it seems as if he just "blows" money. A fun addict is the kind of guy who sees no reason at all to keep a life insurance policy when cashing it in would provide enough money to buy two snowmobiles before the last snow of the season melts. "After all, you said you wanted us to spend more time together," he'll happily explain.

How can you thrive in a marriage to a fun addict? If you are a fun addict, too, then you probably really do enjoy your husband. However, two people who see money only as a means to play can easily come to financial ruin. So, before you go have fun, minimize your chances of poverty: cut up every credit card you have, pay your bills on time, and then play with the remaining cash.

Often, however, it is the serious woman who is drawn to the "very fun" man. If that sounds like your situation, the best you may be able to do is to get the absolute necessities taken care of and then relax. A fun addict is not going to be interested in a budget. However, he may be quite willing to enjoy a certain amount (meaning the most that can be spared, not the least you can possibly agree on) that can be spent any way he wants, whenever he wants, without you rolling your eyes. A fun addict adds zest and perspective to life. Enjoy him.

BEING MARRIED TO THE STATUS SEEKER

A status seeker is always bidding for approval. Voted the one most likely to pick up the check, he always gives the impression that he is running for political office. His goal is approval, but the road there is usually through comparison and competition. The status seeker will wait to sense the direction in which the majority of people are about to go; then he will try to get in front of them.

His perspective is similar to the little boy who announced upon his arrival home from school that he was the leader of his class both to and from the library. "That's wonderful," his parents responded. "How did you get to be the leader?" He looked at them with amazement and responded, "I just walked faster than anyone else." He, like most status seekers, thought leadership had to do with being in front more than it did with guiding.

A status seeker is concerned with impressing people. Therefore, the frustration of being married to a status seeker comes when his spending centers on what will be seen by the public, rather than what will best meet the family's needs. To a status seeker, having a large house on the right street is more important than whether or not he has a good insurance policy. Having the right automobile and the correct label on his clothes can seem as important as the character of the person who has them. The expenditures for the designer items that he insists upon are likely to put a strain on the average income and a strain on you, as his spouse.

Realize that you have the ability to meet his need for approval. Your respect will *not* give him a big head, and your affirmation can go a long way in filling his desire to be esteemed. You certainly approved of him at one point in your relationship or you wouldn't have married him. With enough respectful love, the status seeker might seek the status of being the best husband.

BEING MARRIED TO THE ARTIST

What comes to mind when you hear the word *artist?* Is it some little fellow with a goatee, a beret, a palette of paints and an easel? Reconsider your definition of artist, because you just might be married to one.

The goal of the artist is self-expression. He needs to express what is inside himself to his own satisfaction. An artist is much more concerned with the integrity of his creation than he is its popularity. An artist has a deep drive to leave some mark on the world, some evidence of uniqueness, whether or not other people want it.

If your husband is an artist, he spends practically every

cent he can gather on some kind of special collection: antiques, books, cars, tools, sports, or something that he considers to be significant. Why, you may wonder, would this wonderful man not want to budget some money for the family vacation, the Christmas club, emergencies, or a better car? It is because none of these matter to the artist.

If you are married to an artist, you may find yourself thinking, "I wish he would pay as much attention to me as to those stupid _____." The bad news is that the artist doesn't initially think in terms of people. But there is some good news: If you prioritize the artist's method of expression, and you have recognized his need, he is unlikely to be preoccupied with how you feel the rest of the money should be used.

The world's great inventions come from artists who are more fascinated with what they can produce than with who notices it. Yet, as a wife who is good to her husband on purpose, you learn that noticing is the avenue to romance with the artist. Respect his financial perspective. When you understand his work, you are loving him.

BEING MARRIED TO THE ASPIRING MILLIONAIRE

U.S. News and World Report (February 1989) reported that the typical millionaire is an individual who has worked eight to ten hours a day for thirty years and is still married to his or her high school or college sweetheart. A New York executive research firm, in a study of 1,365 corporate vice presidents, discovered that 87 percent were still married to their first and only spouse. Staying married may not make you a millionaire, but statistically, there is a better chance of becoming one if you stay married than if you don't.

What is it, though, that makes a truly aspiring millionaire for the gold? Not security—if he were interested primarily in security, he would accumulate bits of money into a tidy sum and not take risks to make it big. Not pleasure—if he were interested primarily in pleasure, he would not work hard enough and long enough or invest enough to become a millionaire. Not popular approval—if he were interested primarily in popular approval, he would hand over too much control to other people's opinions. Not self-expression—though aspiring millionaires have more in common with artists than they have with those in the other categories. So what does make an aspiring millionaire tick?

Quite often he is proving that he can accomplish what some significant person (one whom he respects from his past or present) thought he could, or he is proving that he can achieve what that significant person thought he *never* could. It makes no difference whether or not that significant person is still around.

If your husband has this financial philosophy, he will work long hours, may risk the family fortune, and you may live like paupers in order for him to succeed. You must be very patient. Recognize his efforts on your behalf and let him know that you appreciate him.

THE BEST FINANCIAL STEP

It's been said that there are two ways to be rich—one is to have a lot and the other is to not need a lot. There is only one way, though, to be rich spiritually and that is to give a lot. No matter which financial philosophy you or your husband may have, whether or not you have sufficient income, there is one aspect of finances which matters more than any other. That is the biblical principle of tithing. God instructed His people to give the first ten percent (a tithe) of their income.

In a culture where money and possessions are practically worshiped, tithing is a powerful step of faith and an effective way to force your spirit to rely on God. He wants you to give. When you do, you are blessed in various ways. The words from the Lord are strong. Malachi 3:8–10 says:

> "Will a man rob God? Yet you rob me. But you ask,
> 'How do we rob you?' In tithes and offerings. You are

under a curse... because you are robbing me. Bring the whole tithe into the storehouse, that there may be food in my house. Test me in this," says the LORD Almighty, "and see if I will not throw open the floodgates of heaven and pour out so much blessing that you will not have room enough for it."

This passage is the only one in the Bible in which God says, "Test Me."

Tithing starts with an attitude of gratitude and then, supernaturally, the blessings come. To neglect to tell you of this very significant aspect of my relationship with God would be to leave out a very important aspect of that relationship. Thanks to parents who taught me that a penny out of every dime I earned was to be given to God's work, I have tithed since I was very young. Tithing matters. If you already tithe, you know exactly what I mean.

If you decide to take God up on His offer to tithe, agreement on this between you and your husband is important. All of the money you have belongs to both of you. If he strongly opposes tithing, pray that God will change his attitude. There is no reason for you to carry any guilt about it or to sneak money into an offering plate and hope he never finds out. God knows the desire of your heart as well as the constraints that you face.

Perhaps you and your husband agree on tithing—or at least he doesn't object—but you just aren't sure you have the money right now to commit to it. I can assure you that you *cannot* afford to wait. Go ahead; test God—tithe. Give this gift to His work and watch God unwrap the power He intends for you and all of your relationships.

CHAPTER THREE:
FINANCES

MAKING IT PERSONAL

1. What financial philosophy do you think your husband has adopted? What advantages does that philosophy offer?

    _____

    _____

2. What is one decision that you could make about your finances that would please your husband?

    _____

    _____

3. What benefits do you think God may have had in mind when He established the tithe?

    _____

    _____

4. List some practical steps you can take to avoid debt. Or, if you already have incurred debt, list ways you can reduce it.

    _____

    _____

    _____

5. What are some steps you could take to improve the financial situation in your home?

    _____

    _____

    _____

CHAPTER THREE:
FINANCES

- Tell your husband you appreciate all he does to provide for you. Thank him sincerely, face-to-face, and state some of the specifics for which you are grateful.

- Cut up at least one of your credit cards. If you have no credit cards, buy yourself a bouquet of flowers to celebrate your good financial sense.

- Discuss with your husband the principle of the tithe and ask for his agreement to "test God" by tithing for a few months.

Chapter Four

Sleeping Together

A Present Should be Unwrapped

*Love talked about can
be easily turned aside, but love
demonstrated is irresistible.*[1]
—W. Stanley Mooneyham

A great sexual relationship with your husband can add warmth to every aspect of your marriage. However, sex is not the goal of a great marriage; instead, it is a God-given reminder of the uniqueness of the relationship. Sex is not having your way with your husband; it is having a way to get closer to your husband. Scripture states that a man and woman *know* each other through this act of intimacy. "And Adam *knew* Eve his wife; and she conceived, and bare Cain, and said, I have gotten a man from the LORD" (Genesis 4:1, KJV, emphasis added).

Through the Bible, God presented the purposes of a sexual relationship:

TO BE FRUITFUL AND MULTIPLY

> So, God created man in his own image, in the image
> of God he created him; male and female he created

them. God blessed them and said to them, "Be fruitful and increase in number; fill the earth and subdue it. Rule over the fish of the sea and the birds of the air and over every living creature that moves on the ground."

—GENESIS 1:27–28

TO EXPERIENCE A SATISFYING LOVE

Drink water from your own cistern, running water from your own well. Should your springs overflow in the streets, your streams of water in the public squares? Let them be yours alone, never to be shared with strangers. May your fountain be blessed, and may you rejoice in the wife of your youth. A loving doe, a graceful deer—may her breasts satisfy you always, may you ever be captivated by her love.

—PROVERBS 5:15–19

Let him kiss me with the kisses of his mouth—for your love is more delightful than wine. Pleasing is the fragrance of your perfumes; your name is like perfume poured out...

—SONG OF SONGS 1:2–3

Continue reading through the Song of Songs for more of these beautiful expressions of love.

TO PREVENT SEXUAL SIN

But since there is so much immorality, each man should have his own wife, and each woman her own husband. The husband should fulfill his marital duty to his wife, and likewise the wife to her husband.

—1 CORINTHIANS 7:2–3

If you do not understand the mechanics of sex, then get educated. Numerous resources are available on this subject, including several written with a biblical perspective. *Intended for Pleasure* by Ed Wheat and *Celebration of Sex* by Dr. Don E. Rosenau are just two examples. Make sure you have the information you need about your husband's body and your own.

> ***God has given you this incredible way to satisfy your husband. The privilege of bringing him this specific joy has been given only to you.***

Don't let misinformation, personal hang-ups, or past sins cause you to have problems with sex in your marriage. God has given you this incredible way to satisfy your husband. The privilege of bringing him this specific joy has been given only to you.

If you suffer from guilt because you were involved in sexual relationships prior to marriage, it is important for you to realize that your marriage bed does not hold the sin—your head and heart do. Allow God to cleanse these sins from your thoughts and feelings.

> Let us draw near to God with a sincere heart in full assurance of faith, having our hearts sprinkled to cleanse us from a guilty conscience and having our bodies washed with pure water.
>
> —HEBREWS 10:22

Your guilt can be completely replaced with forgiveness when you confess to God.

> If we confess our sins, he is faithful and just and will forgive us our sins and purify us from all unrighteousness.
>
> —1 JOHN 1:9

Marie and John decided to burn their old love letters from past relationships.

BLOWING OUT OTHER FLAMES

Shoeboxes filled with love letters from the guys you didn't marry, tapes and CDs of "your song," old pictures of you and your ex-dates—these are the kinds of things you may keep tucked away. You know the best place for all of that stuff? The trash can. If it has some value and you don't want to throw it away (like a tape or CD or jewelry) then just give it to a charity. Any space, energy, or time you invest in romantic keepsakes should deal only with the relationship between you and your husband.

> *Memorabilia of other loves is a form of infidelity. It can turn from a warm remembrance to a weapon of revenge that burns your partner.*

Memorabilia of other loves is a form of infidelity. It can turn from a warm remembrance to a weapon of revenge that burns your partner. These keepsakes are not simply reminders of where you have been. They provide a place to go when you are dissatisfied with where you are. There is a difference between a pleasant memory that spontaneously occurs from time to time, and a memory that gets your focused attention.

Your husband's jealousy may be sparked by any interest that you have left in old flames. Even jokingly telling your husband to remember, "There are other fish in the sea," may hook his attention, but it is a dangerous line. While jealousy and its accompanying attention give a temporary intensity to the relationship, it is an ineffective substitute for the kind of naturally inspired attention that continually grows. The thrill of a jealous outburst is momentary, and nothing constructive results. Give your husband reassurance that he is, and always will be, your one and only. You may be able to convince him in bed without saying a word.

INFATUATION IS FAKE LOVE

Love happens with a real person—your husband, whom you know inside and out. Infatuation happens with an idealized person—one with whom you fantasize a perfect relationship. Love for your husband will thrive on closeness and knowledge, but distance and ignorance feed infatuation with another. Love emphasizes your husband's dreams and desires. Infatuation emphasizes being in love with the feelings of being in love. In marriage, love takes effort, is realistic and never gives up on its search for all the treasures within your spouse. Infatuation, like a dream, seems to build effortlessly because it is neither limited to nor fed by reality. Love is real and immeasurably valuable; infatuation is its imposter and very cheap. Don't be fooled.

ROMANCE VERSES

Wives love romance, and husbands love sex—at least, that is the reality in many marriages. Ann Landers, a nationally syndicated advice columnist, polled her female readers to learn whether they would be content to be held closely and treated tenderly in lieu of sexual intercourse. More than ninety thousand women responded. Seventy-two percent said they would be content with closeness and tender treatment. Forty percent of those who responded were younger than forty.

If you are one who would also say closeness and tenderness can replace lovemaking, then you can be fairly certain that you feel differently than your husband does about sex. Sexual fulfillment is a man's most basic love need, according to a number of surveys.[2] Armed only with this information, you probably know enough to make your husband a happy man. Love your husband enough to give him your body. It rightfully belongs both to you and to him.

My husband told me he'd rather
have sex than eat...luckily I don't know
how to cook anyway!

The wife's body does not belong to her alone but also to her husband. In the same way, the husband's body does not belong to him alone but also to his wife. Do not deprive each other except by mutual consent and for a time, so that you may devote yourselves to prayer. Then come together again so that Satan will not tempt you because of your lack of self-control.

—1 CORINTHIANS 7:4–5, EMPHASIS ADDED

Do all that you can to let him know you love him. Remember—if your husband is one who can best hear that sentiment in bed (and he probably is), then go to bed.

> ***Do all that you can to let him know you love him. If your husband is one who can best hear that sentiment in bed (and he probably is), then go to bed.***

You may think ambiance in those moments is critical— negligee, music, candles, satin sheets, and sweet perfume. I hate to tell you this, but your husband probably would be equally thrilled if he knew the kids weren't home and he saw you lying naked on the couch. That's the truth! Men are just different.

I WAS JUST THINKING ABOUT ME

If you use lovemaking to elicit a change in your husband's attitude or behavior, that is manipulation. Don't give in to the temptation to do something to benefit him in order to personally benefit. A manipulative wife is not good to her husband *on* purpose; she is good to him *for* a purpose. The difference between those two attitudes is huge. Manipulative behavior is a difficult habit to break, but with God's help, it certainly can be done. Sex is an opportunity to love, so to use it as a means for personal gain is self-centered.

That isn't the only egocentric perspective that can cause problems with lovemaking. A lousy self-image is not always recognized as self-centeredness, but it is. Anytime your focus is on your inadequacies or, for that matter, your competencies, you are centered on self. Either focus can capture your attention and limit your thinking of others. If your self-image comes through the world's understanding of beauty, instead of God's declaration of it, it doesn't matter how "perfect" your body is, you will always focus on its defects and have a poor self-image. Ten years into a marriage, the bride in your wedding album looks different from the woman you face in the mirror. But, whether ten years or sixty years have passed since your wedding day, you are still God's gift to your husband.

Being a wife is about loving your husband, *not* about loving the way your own body looks. To get your husband to overlook any faults in your appearance, distract him with pleasure and allow him the privilege of distracting you with pleasure as well. Go to bed intending to please him, and, as a result, you too will be more satisfied.

> *To get your husband to overlook any faults in your appearance, distract him with pleasure and allow him the privilege of distracting you with pleasure as well.*

Every time you make love with your husband there is a confirmation that you are totally committed to him. Sex is not just icing on the marital cake; it is a basic ingredient of the relationship. If your husband wants to make love, and you just aren't in the mood, making love is probably still your best choice. That response is both logical and thoughtful.

You probably try to meet a variety of your husband's needs with little hesitancy. For example: if your husband

Cora, keeping their 40-year marriage
exciting, has an orthopedic backseat
installed in their car!

says he is cold, but you aren't, that probably doesn't stop you from giving him a sweater; if your husband is hungry, but you aren't, your feelings probably do not prohibit you from sitting down with him for an early dinner. The same principle applies to your sexual relationship. If he wants to make love, but you don't, it would be considerate and sensible of you to respond in a way that is helpful to him.

The only way I know to develop a godly attitude and prevent self-centered thinking about anything, including your sex life, is to pray about it. As peculiar as this may seem, it works. Prayer works for every bad attitude from manipulation to lousy self-esteem, and it works no matter how you acquired the warped perception of yourself. God can give you His perspective because He cares about every aspect of your life.

God created your body. He meant for this aspect of your relationship with your husband to bring joy to both of you. Pray that you will see your body as a gift to your husband and his body as a gift to you. Whether your issues concerning lovemaking with your husband are about where, when, how, or how often—*if there is no contradiction between your husband's preferences and God's instruction*—use prayer to give you the perspective of an on-purpose wife.

FOR BETTER, FOR WORSE—FOR GOOD

There is nothing more devastating to a marriage than infidelity, but in spite of the chaos it causes, there are instances in which adultery is not the ultimate victor. Here is a case in point.

Melissa was married for nearly ten years to Tom, a poster boy for success. While Melissa was frustrated with Tom's frequent business trips, she was never bored while he was away. Her children, family, church, and community involvement kept her very busy. Interacting with many friends helped her pass the time during Tom's long absences. Generally speaking, Melissa coped well when her husband was away. However, when he did spend time at home, her repetitive monologue was clear and consistent—I miss you and want you to be closer to the kids and to me. A wonderful sentiment, but the words she spoke came from a heart filled with great frustration and little gratitude—and that message is the one Tom heard. "For out of the overflow of the heart the mouth speaks" (Matthew 12:34).

To live as a couple became more and more difficult. Individual opportunities were offering them separate directions. When they did occasionally focus on their relationship, she lectured and he "listened" with the hope that the evening might include making love. Beyond these infrequent encounters, neither of them was investing much energy into the marriage.

One warm fall afternoon, the dreaded news arrived. Melissa's busy husband had not been too busy to be involved in a number of sexual affairs. Devastated by the news, Melissa initially decided she could divorce him and even God would understand. "I tell you that anyone who divorces... *except for marital unfaithfulness,* and marries another... commits adultery" (Matthew 19:9, emphasis added).

The days passed slowly, and the nights were insufferable. Melissa thought about life without the man she loved, and she thought about their children being separated from him. The more she thought, the more she recognized that while Scripture gave the option to leave for reasons of adultery, it did not mandate or necessarily encourage it. She believed that God gave her the option of divorce as a way out, but He didn't tell her it was the only way.

Melissa began to pray about her choices. Her prayers focused both on determining what she should do, and on letting God be the one to deal with Tom's infidelity. After a few weeks of prayer and intense, sometimes conflicting, conversations with Christian counselors and friends, she determined that she could not give up on her marriage until she tried to be a wife who purposed to be good to her husband. She felt that God, through her prayer time with Him, was giving her a list of things that she *should* or *could* have done differently in their marriage. She wrote them down and she determined, with God's help, to live from the list for three months. If, after that, her husband committed to remain faithful, she would continue to be his wife. If not, she thought that she would be free of the inner voices haunting her with, "I *should* have, I *could* have..."

Melissa disciplined her life to try this because she had made a commitment to God, as well as to her husband, through her wedding vows. She knew she had promised "for better, for worse" and that also meant "for good." Being married to this man was supposed to be permanent. She decided that any decision to leave him would not be based on anger, exhaustion, or embarrassment. She could file for divorce only when she knew she had really done her best, with God's help.

As one of Melissa's friends, I can personally attest to her character. She is an awesome woman of God. Nothing about her plan concerned manipulating her husband. She was simply disciplining her life to act in the way she felt God was calling her to act—as a gift from Him to her husband.

Tom, on the other hand, was angry and he placed the blame on Melissa. He made certain she knew that this was payback for treating him "so badly for so long." Melissa understood that he was furious about her shortcomings, but even more than that, he was disgusted with himself for the infidelity. Melissa was smart and mature enough to deal only with the part of the problem that she could. She asked Tom's forgiveness for all she had done wrong in their marriage and said she was going to be the wife to him that God had wanted her to be all along.

Her husband didn't buy it. The more godly her actions, the

more he thought she was faking. Temporarily, Tom even became bolder in his infidelity. Melissa really struggled with his attitude. She cried, prayed, and disciplined her life to continue faithfully to honor Tom through her words and actions, in spite of his response. Two months passed before her husband sincerely believed she might actually be changed. Once he became convinced, he acknowledged that the "new" Melissa had to be the result of her relationship with God. Eventually, Tom prayed to have that same relationship with God.

Together, Tom and Melissa made a fresh start. The family moved halfway across the country, and Tom took a job that required virtually no travel. Years later, they continue to honor God and each other. Tom often reminds Melissa that she never needs to worry about him betraying her again. He repeatedly thanks her for her incredibly selfless effort to hold their marriage together. He says her unselfish example—choosing to love him no matter what—brought the reality of what Christ did for him on the cross into focus.

> *It is not about who did the worst thing;*
> *it is about who will do the best thing.*

That true story has a sad, yet common, beginning and a happy, yet uncommon, ending. There certainly is no guarantee of identical results for every woman who tries this. However, the reason there was a happy ending for Tom and Melissa's story is due, in great part, to an incredibly disciplined and godly woman's willingness to attempt to correct her wrongs and love her husband through his. It is not about who did the worst thing; it is about who will do the best thing.

GO, GOING ... STAY?

During the thirty-plus years that my husband has been in full-time pastoral ministry, *every* marital crisis he has seen conclude in divorce has had sexual issues somewhere in the midst of the chaos. In spite of the media's attempts to portray "sleeping around" as no big deal, infidelity is still the ultimate betrayal in a marriage. If you are in the painful situation of loving/hating a husband who strayed, pray, seek good Christian counsel on how to handle the situation, and pray some more. If your husband is remorseful and asks you to give him another chance, there are a million reasons not to do so, but there are also some good reasons to consider giving him another opportunity. Not the least of these is that God forgives and asks us to forgive, "Forgive us ... as we also have forgiven ..." (Matthew 6:12). The decision is yours to make, but do not try to make it alone! You need God's help if you decide to leave your adulterous husband as much as you need His help if you choose to forgive him for past infidelity and start anew. Either course of action is possible—neither is easy.

IF YOU ARE THE ONE
WHO IS TEMPTED

Men and women have affairs for different reasons. Women are usually hoping for love and romance—an emotional connection. Men are usually hoping for sex. I mentioned this in the section about what men and women consider to be important within a marriage, and the point applies equally in the world of affairs.

Passionate interest in a man other than your husband is likely to be an attraction to some quality that you believe your marriage relationship lacks. Don't let loneliness or a shortage of confidence or boredom blur your vision. These problems typically are disguised and may show up in marriage as difficulty with anger management, control issues, or emotional shutdown. Inane soap operas or trashy romance novels—both of which prompt contemplation that is egocentric—can feed your negative emotions.

No matter how the specific details of temptations differ, the problem is always the same—looking away from God for solutions to your pain. Look again to God.

> For we do not have a high priest who is unable to sympathize with our weaknesses, but we have one who has been tempted in every way, just as we are— yet was without sin. Let us then approach the throne of grace with confidence, so that we may receive mercy and find grace to help us in our time of need.
>
> —HEBREWS 4:15–16

Maybe you feel overlooked at home, but you know someone who is looking you over. Maybe you feel limited at home, but you know someone who wants to include you in his boundless adventures. Maybe you feel pressure at home, but you know someone who enjoys you and seems to require little from you. When you begin to think about a man who is not your husband as an alternative for what you are missing in your marriage, get away from him, stay away from him, and do not look back.

> Flee from sexual immorality. All other sins a [woman] commits are outside [her] body, but [she] who sins sexually sins against [her] own body. Do you not know that your body is a temple of the Holy Spirit, who is in you, whom you have received from God? You are not your own; you were bought at a price. Therefore honor God with your body.
>
> —1 CORINTHIANS 6:18–20

Sexual sin starts with thoughts that are followed by action.

> But I tell you that anyone who looks...lustfully has already committed adultery...in [her] heart.
>
> —MATTHEW 5:28

Some people have distorted this Scripture to say that if you have already committed adultery in your heart, you might as well do it with your body. That is ridiculous. This verse is meant to show us that our thoughts alone can put us in need of God's forgiveness.

Your thoughts can affect the way you behave, but they don't have to do so. You have the power to control them, and you do not have to act on them. Don't *do* the wrong thing just because you *think* the wrong thing. Many more lives will be affected by your wrong actions than by your wrong thoughts.

> *Don't do the wrong thing just because you think the wrong thing. Many more lives will be affected by your wrong actions than by your wrong thoughts.*

If you are looking to someone else to fulfill the desires that God meant for your husband to fulfill, your desires are selfish and misplaced. Tell God you are sorry. Prayer can soften your heart toward your husband, and God does not resist an invitation to restore love. Be intentional about making good decisions, and take action to get into a better way of thinking. It is time to respect—"to again look at"—your spouse. You can do this because you vowed to do so on your wedding day, and God heard you. He will help you keep your promises.

If radical action is required, then take it—quit watching your favorite soap opera, stop reading worthless romance novels, and purposely avoid your fantasized "Mr. Perfectly Wonderful." Ultimately, even if it necessitates telling your husband of your sinful desires and then moving your family out of town, do it. Stop the infatuation in your mind before your body joins in the fantasy. As Benjamin Franklin said, "It is easier to suppress the first desire than to satisfy all that follow it."[3]

WHEN YOU FEAR THE MARRIAGE IS LOST

If you or your husband have strayed from the path of fidelity, then stop, get directions, and start again. Before you arrived in this horrible place, you were headed toward a destination together. When one of you strays from the course, the chance of ultimately reaching your goals together is diminished but not impossible.

Several years ago Joel and I were traveling, and we became hopelessly lost. When it became obvious that we were not going to arrive at our destination on time, we pulled into a gas station and asked for directions. The attendant said, "You go up the road to the first stoplight, go to your right and . . . " After he finished giving the directions, including landmarks, we thanked him, pulled onto the highway and braked at the first stoplight. The intersection was quite unique. A right turn could be made onto either of two roads—one that veered slightly in that direction or the other, which quite sharply angled back to the right. We guessed and turned. Several minutes passed and we still had not seen any of the landmarks that the attendant at the gas station had mentioned.

Now we were in a dilemma. Were we better off finding our way from where we were, or going back and choosing the other right turn? Proceeding from the other right turn would give us the advantage of being able to use the directions we had been given, so that was what we did. If we had tried to find our desired destination without going back to what we knew to be a right place from which to start again, we would have become totally lost. We were late, but we did arrive.

If you or your husband have made a wrong turn and have strayed, you can't undo that fact, but proceeding on the wrong road is absurdity. Sometimes the best progress you can make is to return to a place where you *can* make the right choice. Revisit your wedding vows and start again from there. Even if you have to go there first without him, it will keep you from making choices from a place where the perspective is totally wrong.

When a commitment is renewed—again made new—you can truly start again and use God's directions to keep you on your journey together. Only when you or your ex-husband has remarried is it too late to consider this option. Short of that, any couple—even those who have legally divorced— have the opportunity to try again. Commitments can last when "…anyone is in Christ [because] he is a new creation; the old has gone, the new has come" (2 Corinthians 5:17).

That truth is for your own life as well as your husband's. And, since the "two shall become one," it is also true for you as a couple.

CHAPTER FOUR:
SLEEPING TOGETHER

❧❧❧

MAKING IT PERSONAL

1.   What are the biblical purposes of a sexual relationship?

_____

_____

_____

2.   When are you most attracted to your husband? Why? When is he most attracted to you? Why?

_____

_____

3.   What are some practical steps you can take to make the time and have the right mindset to make love with your husband more often?

_____

_____

4.   What are the benefits of your husband's sexual appetite? What are the benefits of yours?

_____

_____

5.   List three ways that love differs from infatuation and determine if there is anyone or anything you need to avoid in order to steer clear of sexual temptation.

_____

_____

_____

CHAPTER FOUR:
SLEEPING TOGETHER

MAKING IT PRACTICAL

- Go to bed naked.

- Take the initiative in making love to your husband.

- Discard any memorabilia you have saved from previous relationships.

Chapter Five

Parental Tactics 101

Tots to Twenties

Children are like wet cement.
Whatever falls on them makes an impression.[1]
—Lillian Sparks

Your marriage can hum along smoothly and then, with only nine months of warning or less, a baby joins in with gurgles and wails. There is no need for this incredible blessing to interfere with the harmony in your relationship; however, a baby often does.

Although being a mom is incredibly rewarding, initially it may be exhausting, worrisome, and isolating—plus you may be stuck with thirty extra pounds that you were sure, before the delivery, were all baby. To lighten these burdens, try napping, spending time in prayer, seeking out other moms, exercising and watching what you eat. These are much better options than the more popular remedy— being mad at your husband.

Resenting your husband is a popular choice because it appears to meet all of your needs at once. You can't yell at a baby, so you yell at him. You can't get out often, so you hold a grudge because he comes and goes as he pleases. You can't seem to get enough sleep, so you make it a point to close drawers and doors a little too loudly when he sleeps. You can't manage to lose the extra weight, so, because you are embarrassed, you resist making love.

These problems are common, and they can quickly change you from a loving partner to the stereotypical, crabby wife. If you have seen changes in your husband since your baby was born, there is a very good chance that those changes are a direct result of changes in you. If you see time with your husband only as a distraction from your baby's needs, or see his advances as insensitivity to your state of exhaustion, he will be frustrated. Here is the hard truth: you will be much happier if you stop attempting to discipline your husband and begin to discipline yourself. You *can* make progress by dealing with just one problem area at a time.

Use what energy you have to improve yourself. For example, if you would be more patient with your responsibilities and sweeter to your mate if you weren't so tired, take a nap. Yeah, right—if you had time to do that, you'd be asleep right now. So maybe the solution for you goes back a step. Perhaps what you really need to do is get more organized, and that would give you some extra time to nap. If, however, you don't have a clue how to get more organized, maybe the solution goes back yet another step. Maybe you need to read a book on how to get organized, put what you learn into practice, and then nap time can be a reality. Or, maybe this sounds so overwhelming that you have decided you aren't all that tired after all.

Initially, change requires plenty of energy. Once you are actually moving through the process, though, you will be refreshed and more confident. Those qualities can go a long way in addressing a real problem.

A HUSBAND IS NOT JUST A GIANT CHILD

One of the greatest gifts you can give your child is to love and respect his father. Always say the best, kindest, most encouraging, truthful things to your child about his dad. Or, worst-case scenario, as your mother used to say, "If you can't say something nice, don't say anything at all."

Your child needs to see your love and respect for his father. He will never forget the way you treat your husband, for better or for worse.

If you choose to treat your husband as if he were another youngster in the family, or usurp his authority in front of your child, you will cause harm to your marriage, and your child's self-concept. Your child needs to see your love and respect for his father. He will never forget the way you treat your husband, for better or for worse. The better you treat your husband, the better your marriage and family dynamics. Positive or negative, all parental encounters are imprinted in a child's memory. Your child is more likely to be a loving respectful spouse if he has witnessed a loving, respectful relationship.

BOYS WILL BE . . .

As her sons jumped on the couch, turned up the television volume as loud as it would go, ransacked the refrigerator, and tossed their popcorn in the air to see "who could juggle the most," my friend just smiled and said, "Boys will be boys."

That phrase—"boys will be boys." I had heard it before, but it bounced around in my head for days after that particular experience. Nothing about that scene looked quite right to me, but, as my friend had graciously pointed out, I didn't have any children—yet. "You'll see," she said.

A few years later our first son was born. As he neared his second birthday, our second son made his appearance. By the time our third son arrived, some three years after that, I thought about that old saying, "Boys will be boys," and I realized it was a lie.

The truth is, boys will be men. And I recognized that if I did not keep that truth in mind, I would be one inept mom. I had seen enough in the lives of my peers to know that when your children are out of control, your whole life is affected. The impact of that on a marriage can be of great consequence.

As my sons grew, I continually reminded myself that each would one day be someone's husband, someone's father, someone's employee, someone's boss, and quite possibly someone's only look at what it means to be a Christian.

Joel and I raised Josh, Isaac, and Joel from a future perspective: we pictured each one as the godly man we hoped he would be. Then we put enough structure into their lives to encourage growth toward that goal.

Only a good and strong foundation can support maturity. For all intents and purposes, the job of raising them had to be completed in eighteen years. That seems to be a short time for all the training a child needs. (Then again, considering the energy required from the parents, it seems to be a very long time.) Having a vision for your child's future is powerful motivation to be faithful and consistent in child rearing through those years. In fact, a vision is more than motivating—it is essential. "Train a child in the way he should go, and when he is old he will not turn from it" (Proverbs 22:6).

HE IS STILL YOUR HUSBAND

When you are raising your children and not just watching them grow up, the task is one of the most fulfilling and exhausting you will ever face. As a result, there is a big temptation to neglect "the other grown up" in the family.

It's easy to think, "I'll get back to my husband when the kids are raised." However, raising children will take 30 to 60 percent of your married life. You can't go AWOL as a wife for all those years.

Throughout the child-rearing years, I had to constantly remind myself that even though I was our boys' mom, I was still Joel's wife. That doesn't sound like something that would require memory herbs, does it? Yet it was easy to think of him as the boys' dad rather than my husband. The busyness of raising children and the urgency of many of their needs sometimes made the important needs of my husband seem less significant. They were not.

> *Raising children will take 30 to 60 percent of your married life. You can't go AWOL as a wife for all those years.*

There are many ways you, too, may be tempted to lose the priority of being a wife during the kids-at-home years. Consider these examples:

Your husband asks you to accompany him on a business trip, but it means making complicated care arrangements for the kids, so you stay home.

He wants the kids in bed at least an hour before your bedtime so the two of you can have time together, but it means getting more organized and remaining committed to a schedule. The children want to stay up so they promise to "be good" and "not bother you and daddy." You think, "What can that hurt?" So, they stay up, but "good" or not, "bother" or not, they make a big difference in your time together.

He hopes you will watch his league softball game, but the kids have swimming lessons at the same time and it would be easier just to sit by the pool than to drive over to the diamond after dropping them off. Besides, you would only be able to watch the first inning. How important can it be to see your husband bat just one time? So you choose to spend the whole time poolside in a beach chair rather than part of the time near the dugout in the bleachers.

There must be a million scenarios that deal with these dilemmas. One of the best things you can do as a wife (and as a mother) is to decide, in advance, that these situations will no longer be dilemmas. Decide to seize the opportunities to include yourself in your husband's activities. When your child sees you honor, respect, and prioritize your relationship with his father, that child is greatly benefited. So think creatively and meet these challenges with a sense of adventure. Make choices that work well for your husband, your child, and you. Try thinking "both/and" instead of "either/or" when you face such a predicament.

MORE AND BETTER TIMES MAY BE JUST AROUND A BEND

Child rearing can be done just about anywhere. That is an important concept to grasp. Try to think of ways you can adjust your life to make more time together with your husband a reality, even while you care for your children.

Over the years I snatched back literally thousands of hours with Joel that could have been lost, because I packed the kids into the car and rode along. In that automobile, while Joel visited congregation members in the hospital or at home, the guys and I played games, read stories, drew pictures for grandparents and missionaries, took naps, ate snacks, etc. The boys and I loved the time together.

Even routines can be interesting when you change the scenery. If designating 8:00 P.M. as family time in the dining room works perfectly in your home, that's great. However, if that's not working out, then adjusting to be accommodating makes much more sense than having no time together.

Choose to build an environment that allows your home to

be an encouraging and peaceful place for your husband, child, and for you. This is not some unattainable dream—you can do this! When you love your husband and discipline yourself to model the life you hope your child will someday choose, it creates a wonderful situation for parenting. These circumstances offer a smooth foundation for the progress of your child's spiritual, educational, and physical development.

"ENVIRONMENTAL PROTECTION" BY MARY AND JOSEPH

Jesus grew in wisdom and stature, and in favor with God and men.

—LUKE 2:52

This Scripture verse gives us the framework for raising godly children. We know from this one verse that Mary and Joseph had placed Jesus in an environment that allowed Him to grow mentally, physically, spiritually, and socially.

It follows then that one of your most important jobs, as a parent, is to make sure your child grows up in an environment that

- is conducive to learning—so that he can grow wise.

- offers limits and challenges—so that he can grow healthy and strong.

- affords opportunities for interaction with God and people.

For your child, the details of what that environment should be are discovered through the study of Scripture, prayer, and wise counsel. When the environment communicates that your child belongs to God, he will know his incredible worth. When the environment emphasizes any other messages, no matter how positive—you are cute, you are clever, you are tough, or you are mine—he will see his value as limited. You are the one best equipped to decide the environmental protection policies for your child. And if you have more than one child, determine the best environment for each one based on the unique personality, gifts, and interests of that child.

EDUCATION MATTERS

Public, private, and home school options for educating your child can leave you feeling like you might not make the right choice no matter which you pick. If you and your husband can agree on the education venue, your marriage will not be impacted like it will be if you and he are not comfortable with the same schooling choice. It is important for you to research the academic, social, spiritual, and physical aspects of each option. Pray about your choices, make your decision, and then remember that God is omnipresent and He loves your child. Even if you aren't totally satisfied with his school setting, he is not in it alone.

As a former teacher I can tell you that schools vary greatly. So just because your child has always attended a public school or always attended a private school, he should not automatically go into the same educational venue if you relocate, or if his local school has significant personnel or policy changes. Consistency is important but not if it means sacrificing a good education.

Choose to build an environment that allows your home to be an encouraging and peaceful place for your husband, child, and for you.

Every year we discussed public, private, and home education options and made our best guess as to which one would be most effective for each son. We based our decision on each one's personality, capability, and spiritual leadership. Even if you don't homeschool, stay involved in your child's education from kindergarten through the early high school years.

Then, as a junior or senior in high school, your child should be gaining some of the freedom within which he will soon operate at college or the workplace. Generally, by that time you will be dealing with a very capable young adult—if you stayed on top of his training prior to his sixteenth birthday.

PHYSICAL ACTIVITY

There are advantages to a child playing and exercising that go beyond just "wearing him out so he'll sleep better." Even at a very young age, unstructured playtimes with friends can teach a lot about making choices, making mistakes, and making friends. Get your child into a setting where he can get some exercise and interact with other kids often and regularly.

Organized sports are a fantastic way to teach a son or daughter about rules, good sportsmanship, teamwork, discipline, and more. Sports teams offer a very natural way for you and your husband to be involved in your child's life as he interacts in community. Many marriages would undergo less stress if moms could keep all of that in mind as they wait for their children's bumps, bruises, and breaks to heal.

> *Sports teams offer a very natural way for you and your husband to be involved in your child's life as he interacts in community.*

I know that there are some great moms who are on the sidelines yelling at their kids to "go for it," even if it means risking life and limb, but if sports risks are a challenge for you, I can truly identify. My husband and I had some significant differences concerning our sons' involvement in sports. His motto was, "If it doesn't kill you, it will make you stronger." Mine was, "Safety first." During the eighteen

Tom had mixed feelings when Tiffany finally agreed to let Timmy play football.

years we had one or more boys in athletics, we watched them play a dozen different sports. Naturally, I encouraged them to consider the low-impact options, such as tennis and swimming. I can't adequately tell you of my dismay and Joel's elation when their sports of choice were ultimately football, wrestling, and soccer. I prayed so hard that I needed kneepads in the bleachers!

When a child is a member of a team, he learns principles that can be of worth to him the rest of his life. Initially, his thrill might be to wear a real uniform; but there is potential for long-term happiness in the values he learns while he wears it. Listen to his comments after practices and games to find out whether he is grasping the values. Coach him toward maturity. That means taking the time to give explanations when he has an apparent lack of understanding. Here are some examples:

Your child says, "My coach made me shake the winners' hands and say, 'Good game.' So I squeezed their hands as hard as I could." Your child has given you a wonderful invitation to talk about good sportsmanship.

Your child announces, "Frank should have passed to me—I was wide open! I told him next time he's wide open I'm not throwing him the ball." It's time to review the concept of teamwork.

When others don't play fair, help him understand how making exceptions to rules affects others. Consider it an opportunity for that chat when he complains, "I had that guy pinned—both shoulder blades were on the mat—but the ref wouldn't call it. Bill told me he heard that the kid I was wrestling was the ref's neighbor."

You can discuss the value of discipline and how lack of it affects others if he complains, "We had to run laps for half the practice today just because coach overheard Bill cuss—like my running around a track is gonna do anything to change Bill."

Sports present you with opportunities to have some of your best conversations. And, as a pleasant side effect, they do "wear him out so he sleeps better."

HELPING YOUR KIDS COME TO LOVE GOD

Kids who see consistent love and a Christian lifestyle lived out in their homes are at an advantage because they will try to figure out who God is and how He relates to them. For this reason and others, pray each morning before you lift your head from your pillow. It makes an amazing difference during the day if you spend time with God immediately after waking up. You will feel like you "have it together," in the best sense of that phrase. "I can do everything through him who gives me strength" (Philippians 4:13). So, set your alarm early. You will not regret it. In fact, you are likely to find that you aren't even as tired during the day as you are when you skip the quiet time with God. Prioritize Christ in your home and model the life you hope your child will choose for himself.

Prioritize Christ in your home and model the life you hope your child will choose for himself.

No matter what your child's age or attitude, your prayers will make a difference in a decision for faith in Jesus Christ. Your request opens up a pathway and invites God to reach down and do what He really wants to do. You are an intercessor to the Lord for your child, and He is on your side. He wants your child to come to Him; He loves him even more than you do.

In Exodus 20:5–6, God told us He punishes up to three and four generations of those that hate Him and shows love to a thousand generations of those who love Him and keep

His commandments. A specific pattern of sin may continue, passed on from the parent to the child, not only because it has been modeled, but also because, as a parent, you may feel especially hypocritical holding a child accountable for some of the very things you did or didn't do at his age.

Do not let past sin in your life make you feel unworthy to challenge your child to a godly lifestyle. Your shortfalls should not be a hindrance in your ministry to him. Tell him the pain that your foolishness caused you and how you hope he will never have to experience the ramifications of those kinds of behaviors.

There are parents who say, "Well, what can I expect? I took drugs, drank alcohol, had premarital sex, cheated, lied, and hated God when I was growing up, and I turned out OK. I guess he will just have to find out for himself, like I did." That is ridiculous logic.

Do these same parents say, "I stuck a knife in a toaster, put my hand on a hot stove, and tried to ride a wild boar when I was young. I was electrocuted, badly burned, and almost gored to death—but I'd better let my kid make those same mistakes so he can learn for himself"? No. Those stories get told, and warnings get shared, as they should. Everyone readily agrees that good parents do everything in their power to keep their child from physical harm. How much more ought we to be concerned about a child's spiritual well-being?

Use at least the same proportion of power to prevent your child from sin that you would use if he were planning to jump off of a building—because either can leave scars of regret. Warn of the dangers of bad choices and encourage him to do right because it matters to God. If your husband joins you in warning and encouraging—great. If he does not, that's OK. Continue to respect your husband and relax in the knowledge that God is using his response in the life of your child, too. A child learns something very valuable in seeing you honor your husband—something that he can't learn from your attempts to get his dad to say and do a certain thing.

CHURCH MATTERS

Church is essential in helping a child grow spiritually. That might seem like a given, but I have discovered that it is not. Nearly everyone has heard a horror story about some person who was continually forced to go to church as a child, and, as a result of this "torture," that person has now sworn off church forever, declared war against his family and society, and still lives in constant fear of anything beginning with the letter *C*—all because he had to go to church.

If you are adamant that your child must brush his teeth but don't make him go to church, you give a very powerful message to your child—your teeth matter more to me than your relationship with God and the people who love Him.

I always wonder if, as children, those same individuals were forced to brush their teeth and bathe. If so, do they now refrain from personal cleanliness because of their insensitive parents' values?

A good parent makes a child do things that he or she considers critical for the child's well being. If you are adamant that your child must brush his teeth but don't make him go to church, you give a very powerful message to your child—your teeth matter more to me than your relationship with God and the people who love Him. It is as important to promote consistency and thoroughness in your child's spiritual life as it is in his physical life.

Even though you may totally agree with me philo-sophically, the practicality of getting children out the door on time for church can be daunting. Something that worked very well with our sons, even into their early teen years, was the guaranteed stop by a donut shop on the way to worship, *if* everyone was showered, dressed, and in the car on time. If one of them was just goofing around and time was closing in, his brothers became the motivators, and I avoided much frustration.

Even a toddler benefits from going to a Sunday school class. Being with teachers who are wonderful models of Christian character and meeting other children whose parents are also interested in spiritual growth does make a difference in your child's world. It is important for your child to get to know other people who love God and hold the same values you do. Additionally, parenting is exhausting and the church family is a great place to find support.

If your husband does not go to church, take the children to church by yourself and continue to show your husband respect. Invite him to join you, but don't whine about it. He knows it is important to you—he sees you make the effort to go. If your husband goes to a different Christian church than you and your child, join him at his church to worship together. This is a way to honor him as the spiritual leader of your family, while accomplishing much more for your relationship and for your whole family than would attending your preferred church without him.

If you are a new Christian and you try to initiate a devotional time or attend church for the first time with your teenager, he may think that you've become a religious fanatic (heaven forbid). Find out if there is anyone he knows from school who attends a church, or if there is a Christian youth group in your neighborhood, or whether there is a Christian camp that has a theme or activity that would interest him. Another great way to start a conversation naturally about spiritual things is to respond to his problems or concerns with, "I will be praying for you." God will

Getting to the milk was a challenge after Rick and Roxane started taking their preschooler to Sunday School.

provide the window of opportunity that you need to get this started in your family.

FAMILY DEVOTIONS—PRAYER

> Until now you have not asked for anything in my name. Ask and you will receive, and your joy will be complete.
>
> —JOHN 16:24

Because you want the time to be important and special, family devotions can feel almost austere. This is true whether it is you and your husband, or you and your children, or your entire family that has come together to pray. In an attempt to grow deeper, such a serious tone can be set that devotions feel unnatural or forced. We found that the more natural the circumstances were, the better our sons responded. As a result, the method of our daily family devotions was different during each stage of their development.

Our daily time together, though, has always ended with us (a.k.a., whoever is home at the time) kneeling, seated on the couch, lying on the floor, or standing—whichever is most comfortable for staying focused during prayers. Then from oldest to youngest, we pray out loud. (Joel and I still do this and as our sons visit in our home with their families or friends, they readily join us.)

If any one of us is angry or frustrated, he or she still prays out loud, although sometimes the prayer of that person is rather brief. Since we have always made it clear that this is a time to talk to God and not a time to deal with issues or people, exemption from prayer because of temper is not an option. On rare occasions we sat for a long while in silence, and a few times we all had to pray out loud for the person who was mad before he was willing to pray. The reason for this perseverance is found in Ephesians 4:26, "'In your anger do not sin': Do not let the sun go down while you are still angry."

Occasionally it has been necessary to clarify the purpose of prayer. Here is an example: Isaac, who was eleven at the time, prayed, "Dear God, please help Mom to know she is really being ridiculous about this and make her let me go to Jeff's overnight." This was simply a continuation of a disagreement that he and I had—except now it was disguised as a conversation with God so that I could overhear. I interrupted, "Hey! You are fake praying—start over!"

Be ready, though, because children trained like this will quickly recognize the same flaws in your prayers. I was caught the night I prayed that the boys would please make their beds without me reminding them. The good news is that when I was caught, I knew that they were listening to my prayers!

FAMILY DEVOTIONS—ACTIVITIES

All Scripture is God-breathed and is useful for teaching, rebuking, correcting and training in righteousness.
—2 Timothy 3:16

When the boys were very young we used a picture Bible and Bible character coloring books to emphasize the people of the Scripture and their wonderful stories. Additionally, as Josh, Isaac, and Joel grew, they learned many songs that became a part of the foundation of their faith.

Through song lyrics they learned the books of the Bible, the Ten Commandments, the fruit of the Spirit, and the Lord's Prayer, as well as stories filled with godly principles. Many songs were acted out by a puppet drawn on a hand or by the brothers pretending to be actors on a stage.

Most children—about the time they reach the age of nine or ten—love competition. Did I ever take advantage of that stage! You can, too, by having Bible quizzing or memory competitions followed with prizes ranging from staying up ten minutes longer to getting a new Christian T-shirt, CD, book, or video.

One other activity that kept our boys searching in their Bibles was the refrigerator memory verse. They each took turns finding the verse they wanted us all to memorize.

Every Sunday I posted the new verse on the refrigerator. So, not only were they spending time looking in the Bible for the verse they wanted everyone to learn, they were also memorizing a verse each week.

This choose-and-post-a-verse activity also helps a child realize that some Bible verses can stand alone and greatly impact a life while others desperately need a context. An example of a chosen verse that needed no context was, "All Scripture is God-breathed and is useful for teaching, rebuking, correcting and training in righteousness" (2 Timothy 3:16). An example of a verse, isolated from the rest of the chapter, that did little to impact our daily lives was a paraphrased version of Genesis 25:25—"Esau was a hairy man." Yet it, too, was quite memorable and is still occasionally quoted with a smile.

Recognize your husband as spiritual leader in your home by doing whatever you can to creatively include him without pressuring him to fulfill your agenda.

The best way to help your child grow through devotional times is to use his interests to help him learn more about God. If you are faithful and consistent in your attempts, God uses your efforts in ways that will surprise you.

Don't be exasperated if your husband, a.k.a. the spiritual leader of your family, is often gone during devotional time or simply chooses not to participate. There are many ways that you can include him in what the children are learning. For example:

- Have them give their dad pictures they have drawn of the Bible story characters.

- Ask one child to be a news reporter and have him interview his siblings as they pretend to be a biblical figures or share their thoughts about the Bible lesson. Record the interview and then let the children give the tape to their dad to listen to while he is driving to work.

- Encourage your child to write a Bible verse on one side of an index card and to draw an illustration on the opposite side. Then let him put that card somewhere special for Dad (bathroom mirror, dash of the car, computer monitor, etc.).

Recognize your husband as spiritual leader in your home by doing whatever you can to creatively include him without pressuring him to fulfill your agenda.

KEEP ON KEEPING ON 'EM

"I'm really worried," said one little boy to a friend. "Mom works hard every day washing and ironing, cleaning up after me, taking care of me when I get sick."

His friend asked, "What have you got to worry about?"

"I'm afraid she might try to escape."

It may be the most difficult thing you do in your life, but there is no better way to let a child know you really love him than to *stay the course and continue to parent for eighteen years.* Then, when it actually is time to move to the sidelines of his life (and there really is such a time), you will be able to cheer for the man or woman your child has become.

Ms. Lillian, as President Jimmy Carter's mother was commonly known, was interviewed on television in 1980 while one son was serving in the White House and another, her fourth and youngest child, Billy, was again making headlines as a goofy, beer-guzzling redneck.

The interviewer asked her, "To what do you attribute the differences in your sons?"

Ms. Lillian looked the curious man in the eyes and said, "By the time I got to Billy, I was just plumb wore out."

I am forever in debt to Ms. Lillian for that candid response. The necessary determination came to me every time I thought about the results of quitting before it was time.

Proverbs 22:6 says, "Train a child in the way he should go, and when he is old he will not turn from it." Raising a child takes great investments of thought, time, energy, and money. However, you will find that it takes much less of each of these if you make these investments consistently as he is growing up. If you do little as he grows and then try to "fix" it after he has reached adulthood, the necessary investments are staggering. "No, no," is often the only input that is needed for a two-year-old to change his ways. If however, "no" is seldom said and only randomly enforced as the child grows, then bars and chains may be needed to accomplish the same thing in the life of that sadly neglected child who has grown old, but not up.

DUTIFUL DISCIPLINE

The rod of correction imparts wisdom, but a child left to itself disgraces his mother.

—PROVERBS 29:15

Discipline without support is cruelty, and support without discipline creates weakness. Discipline is what moves a child from self-will to God's will, and that happens in stages. First, your children must learn to obey you. God says so. "Children, obey your parents in the Lord, for this is right" (Ephesians 6:1). God assigned to you this position of authority in their lives, so whether or not you desire the position, you are their boss.

Discipline is not something you do to a child, it is something you do for a child.

You need to know how to set limits, which behaviors to prohibit, and when to punish. "Do not exasperate your children; instead, bring them up in the training and instruction of the Lord" (Ephesians 6:4). When you accept these responsibilities and are consistent in disciplining your child, your discipline will be effective. Disciplining and loving are not contradictory activities. Discipline is not something you do *to* a child; it is something you do *for* a child.

CORRECTION AT HAND

Nearly everyone debates whether or not a parent should spank a child. Traditionally, that is *one* use of the rod of correction. A light smack on a little one's bottom *administered immediately when he is doing something dangerous* can help him learn to avoid those situations. A whack on the behind (never to be administered in anger) often can accomplish immediate behavior improvement in your toddler or preschool child.

"Just wait until we get home...," is not a solution for a very young child's misbehavior, even in a social setting, because he won't connect the discipline with the misconduct if very much time lapses. Therefore, you may try to whisk him away to the closest private place (often a restroom), explain why you are going to spank him, and administer the spanking with your open hand—the ever-ready rod of correction. Always follow up discipline by reiterating why you had to punish him and by reminding your child that you only do so because you love him too much to let him misbehave.

There is a valuable spiritual lesson to be learned through this form of discipline. Wrong choices have unpleasant consequences. He can learn that though you forgive him and continue to love him, disobedience results in pain.

The rod of correction is effective only when better behavior results from its use. Spanking will not always produce better behavior, but that doesn't mean the metaphorical rod of correction should be tossed aside. The rod of correction is not confined to a physical instrument. It is also a metaphor for effecting behavior changes in your child.

Think of all the things for which a rod can be used: to guide, to place a boundary, to prod, to protect or to point to out what is important. Each of these uses could effectively encourage better behavior. The key to successful discipline is not consistently using the same method throughout the child's life, but is consistently responding to his mis-behavior in ways that cause him to behave properly. Don't limit yourself to the physical use of the rod; try various applications of the metaphorical rod of correction.

A ROD OF CORRECTION HAS MANY USES

Once your child is in elementary school, you are past the stage where a smack on the bottom is helpful. Instead, use the rod to guide your child. Restrict him from danger by setting limits and boundaries, but also allow him to make many of his own choices within those boundaries. As he grows older, a child's decisions to obey you are largely reflections of his respect for you. So, it is important that you stayed invested in his very young life. If you are fair and want the best for him, he knows it.

A child this age generally wants to please his parents and others in authority. This is typically a pleasant stage of childhood that affords you a reprieve from the physical exhaustion that came with caring for a toddler and the mental exhaustion you will experience when they are teens. I don't say that to discourage you in any way but only to alert you to enjoy the hiatus.

As your child becomes an adolescent and young teen, use the rod of discipline to prod and protect. Your child probably knows what he is supposed to be doing by this age, but he may be tempted to be non-productive or choose to spend time with "the wrong crowd." Prod him to better himself and his world through practice, service, and learning. Protect him from wrong people and places by sticking to preset, often-discussed guidelines. ("No, you may not go walk around in the mall for five hours even if everyone you know will be there.")

A child this age is going through many physical changes and is beginning to grasp abstract reality. During this time he may have a revelation that, in addition to being his parent, you are also a person. He is now capable of recognizing the results of your relationship with Christ and may begin to desire that life for himself.

He may or may not want you to think that he is interested in developing his spiritual life. Either way, bear in mind that there may never be a more critical time for him to see you faithfully "walk your talk." Because of the stage of life you and your husband are in at this time of your child's development, you may experience temptations you have never faced before. Don't lose perspective, stay focused, and keep your priorities straight—God, husband, children, family, community.

When your child is an older teen, if you have stayed invested since his birth, the very difficult part of parenting is complete. Now the purpose of the rod is only to point continually toward God. Use it to remind your adult child where he can find all that he needs for the rest of his life. When his goal is to live a life that pleases God, he is mature.

CHEERING
THEM UP AND ON

All the strength it takes to raise a child is needed to let him go when he becomes an adult. But, again, if you keep your priorities—God, husband, children, family, community—in proper order, you will have no regrets as your offspring moves out to live on his own.

When that time comes, take a seat in the bleachers and enjoy the rest of his life. You learn in the bleachers that you can't protect your child from mistakes or disappointments.

You learn too that you are no longer his director, coach, or trainer. Your job is now to let go. You may be tempted to shout hints, but you recognize that your opinions have become more distraction than instruction. So, assume the position you will have in his world for the rest of your life: cheerperson.

> ### *When your older teen's goal is to live a life that pleases God, he or she is mature.*

This dynamic is healthier for him, and it sets you free. One of the central truths of love is that each person is ultimately responsible for himself. Your job in middle management between your adult child and God can be eliminated, and you can take a new position. That is an especially tough lesson for parents to learn. The panoramic view from the bleachers, though, makes it more evident. You learn that you are not the owners of your offspring. You never were—they belong to God.

This is a biblical concept called stewardship. A steward is someone who has been honored by being entrusted with someone else's wealth. The steward's job is to manage and develop that treasure until the Master can return to manage it directly. When you say *"my* kid" you should mentally add the phrase "for awhile." Because once your child is mature, he is responsible—"able to act in response to" whatever life brings. As a Christian mom, your job is to help him mature so that he is capable and desirous of a relationship with God and people. When that is accomplished, you can thank God for the incredible privilege you have had in raising him, and then you begin the third season of your marriage. This is a time of encouragement where you witness the fruits of your labors. Proverbs 17:6 reflects on this stage of life, "Children's children are a crown to the aged, and parents are the pride of their children."

CHAPTER FIVE:
PARENTAL TACTICS 101

✦

MAKING IT PERSONAL

1. Name three ways you can prioritize your relationship with your husband while you raise your (tots to twenties) children.

    _____

    _____

    _____

2. In what ways are you tempted to treat your husband like a child? How can you stop doing those things? What are some alternate reactions and behaviors that will show him respect and love?

    _____

    _____

    _____

3. What is the goal that you and your husband have in raising your children?

    _____

4. What would your children say your priorities are? Would what they say differ from what you would say your priorities are?

    _____

    _____

5. After the children are grown, you should seldom give input, unless asked. How can you prepare now for this time?

    _____

    _____

MAKING IT PRACTICAL

- Tell your children something great about their dad every day.

- Help your children make or do something special for their dad.

- Pray for your children and spend time reading the Bible with them daily.

Chapter Six

Communication Matters

Listen . . . Up

*Abigail Van Buren says
at the top of her list of the ten most
common problems she sees in Dear Abby letters is:
"My wife doesn't understand me."*[1]

*Y*ou have many ways to communicate with your husband. However, the effectiveness of each is dependent on you spending significant time in prayer. In *The Power of a Praying Wife,* Stormie Omartian, reveals the miraculous way that a disciplined prayer can alleviate heartache and sustain unity. She states that a marriage's success depends upon "laying down all claim to power in and of yourself, and relying on God's power to transform you, your husband, your circumstances, and your marriage."[2] I couldn't agree more.

I refer you to the inspiration and challenges in Omartian's book because I want to spend the rest of my time with you considering practical ways to communicate with your husband. First of all, make sure you have something good to say. God is in the business of changing hearts, and when He changes yours, your communication will be different.

> The good [woman] brings good things out of the good stored up in [her] heart, and the evil [woman] brings evil things out of the evil stored up in [her] heart. For out of the overflow of [her] heart [her] mouth speaks.
>
> —LUKE 6:45

After you intentionally listen to God, practice listening to your husband on purpose. In the American culture, the emphasis of communication is on giving or receiving information. There are cultures in which connection is the basis for the interchange. We can learn something from them. The greeting of East Africans is a perfect example of communicating connection. In that part of the world, when someone says, "How are you?" the other replies, "I am well, if you are well." Through that answer, even a passer-by knows someone is trying to identify and connect with him. It is clear that someone cares. Understanding is much easier when you really care about the person with whom you are communicating. So, the more you care about your husband, the more likely you are to truly connect with him.

COMMUNICATION FAILURE

> I know you believe you understand what you think I said, but I'm not sure you realize that what you heard is not what I meant.[3]
>
> —RICHARD NIXON

There is no getting around it; communicating is difficult. Any time two people talk, there are several opportunities for communication problems. In a conversation, misunderstanding can result at any one of the following points:

- your intended comment
- your actual comment
- what the listener thinks he hears
- the listener's comment about your comment
- your understanding of the listener's comment about your comment

The following, intended to be polite interaction, illustrates these possible complications:

- your intended comment—
I sure am in the mood to watch a movie.

- your actual comment—
If you don't stop channel surfing I think I'm going to lose my mind.

- what the listener thinks he hears—
You are incredibly irritating.

- the listener's comment about your comment—
You just need to relax; you are always uptight and tense about little stuff.

- your understanding of the listener's comment about your comment—
You are a grouch.

Here, a simple request became a conversation that has your husband feeling accused of being an irritation and you assuming that he thinks you are a grouch. It is highly unlikely that either of you would ask for any clarification after such an interchange. Given the possibilities for misinterpretation and assumed accusation, no wonder communication issues are at the center of many struggling marriages.

LISTEN LONGER

[She] who answers before listening—that is [her] folly and [her] shame.

—PROVERBS 18:13

My husband talks a lot. He preaches a minimum of seven times every week, teaches classes, and interacts with individuals throughout most of every day. Though he does talk throughout so much of the day, by the time he gets home, he is generally "just plumb out of words."

I also talk a lot. The difference is, I seem to be full of

words. No matter what I've done in a day or how many people I've interacted with, there is a seemingly endless supply of words bubbling over the surface of my lips. When I lie down at night, it seems to accelerate their escape.

> *Given the possibilities for misinterpretation and assumed accusation, no wonder communication issues are at the center of many struggling marriages.*

Many women experience this same condition. Like me, you may assume that if your husband wants to interject something into the evening's monologue, he knows he is welcome to do so. But, until then, we talk and our husbands (sometimes) listen.

One evening shortly after we moved from Indiana to Florida, Joel and I decided to take a long walk through our neighborhood. Earlier in the day, I had been taken aback by the sight of a woman using very animated gestures, apparently lecturing her husband as they waited in their car for the traffic light to change. She looked frazzled, he looked dazed, and I looked at my life. I realized that when I talked endlessly to Joel, I probably had the same countenance as the animated woman. I decided right then that I wasn't going to do that anymore. I was going to try to be quiet more often and very purposefully listen to Joel—even if all I heard was his breathing. If there were gaps in the conversation, I decided I would spend the quiet time praying for him instead of incessantly talking *at* him.

As we walked that evening, it wasn't long before he asked why I was so quiet. I told him my observation. He said, "Well, that's nice, but I like to hear you talk. It doesn't bother me. I'll tell you if I want to say something." I learned something I didn't know—he likes to hear me talk! Isn't that amazing. We had been married nearly fourteen years and I never knew how he felt about my chatter.

I told him how much his answer meant to me, and then I was quiet again. About ten minutes silently passed. Then he started to tell me about his day. I was so excited about him talking that I actually interrupted him to thank him. Then I began telling him some of the unusual parts of my day. A half a block later during our walk I realized what I had done. Not only was I not listening again, but I was also interrupting him! It took all of my willpower just to shut up, but when I did, it wasn't too long before he was telling me about his hopes and dreams for the ministry efforts of the church.

God Himself had to seal my lips to keep me from blurting out the questions of how those dreams might move to reality. But there would be time in the future for those to be addressed. So, thanks to His grip on my lips, I was able to listen to Joel as he then reversed the direction of our conversation and took me with him down memory lane.

We walked and he talked about childhood experiences; why he sold his motorcycle while he was in seminary; and how he felt when God was calling him and us to a place far from our roots. He described how much it meant to him when I said the boys and I would "follow him anywhere." Our stroll finally ended, and I was a committed to listening more and talking less.

> When words are many, sin is not absent, but [she] who holds [her] tongue is wise.
>
> —Proverbs 10:19

Since that wonderful evening, Joel and I have had many times together where I listened to him share his thoughts and many other times that I just listened to him breathe. I have learned much about him and about us by praying and listening. I am still full of words, but I have learned that some of them should just stay inside me. If and when they are needed, they will be available for quick retrieval. Isn't it ironic that there is *much to be said* for *saying much less!*

> If anyone considers [herself] religious and yet does not keep a tight rein on [her] tongue, [she] deceives [herself] and [her] religion is worthless.
>
> —JAMES 1:26

WHAT *ARE* YOU THINKING?

There is a story about a husband and wife who were celebrating their golden wedding anniversary—fifty years of married life. Having spent most of the day with relatives and friends at a big party given in their honor, they were back home again. They decided, before retiring, to have a little snack of tea with bread and butter. It was one they had shared many evenings over the years.

They went into the kitchen where the husband opened up a new loaf of bread and handed her the end piece (the heel), whereupon she exploded. She shouted, "For fifty years you have been dumping the heel of the bread on me! I will not take it anymore—this lack of concern for me and what I like!" On and on she went in the bitterest of terms, complaining about the heel of the bread.

The husband was absolutely astonished at her tirade. When she finished, he said to her quietly, "But, my dear, the heel is my favorite part."

Be honest with your husband. You are his partner. Don't let a wrong impression of what you like or what you think cause resentment between you. Tell him your heart, but forego the temptation to do so angrily or repeatedly.

"Everyone should be quick to listen, slow to speak and slow to become angry" (James 1:19). If you are frustrated about something, before you say what you are thinking, ask yourself, "Would I be glad I said this to him even if he died tomorrow?" You can double-check your decision by asking yourself, "Would I want him to say this to me?" If the answer to either of those questions is no, figure out another way to let go of your frustration. And just a reminder: devouring chocolate, guzzling wine coolers, heading for the mall, or phoning peers to say bad things about him are not good ways to release your frustration. Instead, pray, even if you have to force yourself to do so. You probably won't feel like it right then, but God loves time with you—frustrations and all.

NAGGING, SILENCE

"If you don't know, I'm not going to tell you." This attitude makes absolutely no sense. Why in the world would you not tell your husband something you are convinced he should already know? If he says he doesn't know it and you think he should know it, tell him and then he *will* know it. Answer his question and be polite about it. After that, you two can have a conversation that makes sense.

I have known couples who play this ridiculous game for weeks. As the days pass, the anger grows. If you interact this way with your husband and he doesn't think it's fun, then stop it. Just tell the man you love and married whatever it is he says he wants to know. Otherwise, your secret will act like a black hole in your marriage—sucking everything that matters into it.

Nagging is the opposite of the silent treatment—"If I've told you once, I've told you a thousand times…" You may choose this as your verbal assault weapon because you think it is the only way you can "make him do something." You know what? It's not your job to *make* him do anything. Your job is to be your best self, do all you can, say what you think (just once), and then watch what God does in your husband's life and in your relationship.

The silent treatment will not make your relationship with your husband better, and nagging may be even worse than the silent treatment. Proverbs 27:15 says, "A quarrelsome wife is like a constant dripping on a rainy day." And that isn't the only scripture that leaves us with the impression that nagging has been a preferred tactic of many wives for centuries. Nagging can sound like whining or arguing or filibustering, but its results are always the same—frustration for both parties.

Once your husband has the information you are trying to relay, your communication is complete. In other words, if you said it, and he heard you, then you are nagging if you say it again. Why tell him again what he already knows? No doubt you are thinking, "Because his words or actions indicate that he is not responding to what I said."

> *Once your husband has the information you are trying to relay, your communication is complete.*

Let's imagine a simple scenario—one with which most of us are familiar. You say, "Could you take out the garbage?" He says, "Sure, after the game is over." Two hours after the final score has been announced the garbage bag is still sitting in your kitchen. If you are not satisfied because some follow-up was a necessary part of his response, you still have solution options: adjust your timetable, ask if you could help him with it, do it yourself, or hire someone to get it done. These responses will all accomplish the goal of your communication. Getting irritated, yelling, and making demands just says, "You and this relationship matter less to me right now than getting the garbage out of the house."

Maybe you're trying to communicate about something much more significant than the location of the garbage, and you feel justified in "getting on his case." Stop and think: Does this issue matter to you more than he or your relationship with him does, even for a moment?

HIS ACTION/YOUR REACTION

If you feel as if he just doesn't help enough around the house (or with the kids or with the finances or whatever) then tell him what feels overwhelming to you, and let him know you would appreciate his help. Unless you tell him that, he may think you have it all under control, while you assume he should know you need assistance.

When he does help, make sure you don't "fix" what he has already done. Many women are tempted to redress a child (*Why would he dress Sammy in a plaid shirt with those polka-dot pants?*); rescour the bathtub (*Can't he tell he missed all the sides?*); or go to the grocery store again to get the "right" brand of soup (*How can he not know which kind we eat by now?*). Every time you correct his efforts, you communicate that his response is not adequate. He may begin to sense that, in fact, he is not adequate. Once he is convinced that you have that little respect for his hard work, he will give up trying to respond.

The only times you should fix what he has already done is if he asks you to or if tragedy will strike if you don't. Otherwise, leave it alone, thank him for his time and energy, and get on with life.

BUT I WANTED THE RED ONE

The principle of not correcting your husband's efforts (unless not doing so would be catastrophic) holds true for gift exchanges as well. If your husband takes the time to choose a special gift for you, unless it is broken or will cause harm, keep it. If you are in the habit of returning his gifts and "he's fine with that," then I'm guessing there is a good chance he became "fine with that" the first time you communicated the following: "You are a lousy present-chooser, but I will remedy that tomorrow at the store."

If you married a practical thinker, he may never again spend time pondering what you would like. He would perceive that to be a waste of his time. So, while you are convinced he puts no thought or effort into buying for you, he is convinced he is not wasting his time before you head to the mall for the gift exchange. If your husband takes the time to choose something especially for you, treasure it. It is tangible evidence of your special place in his heart.

DEALING WITH THE WEIGHTIER ISSUES

Questions are often recommended as a way to start a conversation. You may see a question as a way to get closer to your husband, but chances are he will assume that you just need an answer to your question—a solution to your problem. This difference in expectations can cause big misunderstandings.

You may ask your husband a question simply to give him an opportunity to say something that will make you feel more secure. But your husband, thinking your question can't possibly have such an obvious answer, may focus on giving you a "correct" response.

Let's say that you ask, "Do you love me?" and he responds, "I married you, didn't I?" It is quite likely that he thinks he gave you facts to provide you with confidence to move on, but you may think he is trying to avoid saying that he loves you.

Some questions you ask, though, may be phrased in a way that masks your real inquiry and makes it nearly impossible for him to give you a satisfactory reply. At moments like these, as your silence demands a response, your husband enters into a dimension of time and space where there are no right answers, but, in spite of that, he knows he has to find one—quickly!

Case in point—if you say to your husband, "You know, if I lost a little weight, I think I'd look a lot better. What do you think?"

The following are three responses to that question that might sound right to him, and each option *is* much better than, "Yeah, you would look better if you weren't so fat."

However, none are likely to sit well with you if you aren't purposefully looking for the best possible interpretation of his answer.

YOUR QUESTION

"Do you think I would look a lot better if I lost a little weight?"

HUSBAND'S RESPONSE OPTION #1

"You're perfect for me just like you are!"

To him this response sounds like an expression of genuine, unconditional love, but what you may hear is, *You're fat, but I don't mind.*

HUSBAND'S RESPONSE OPTION #2

"Well, you look pretty good to me, but if you want to go on a diet, I'm here to support you. I'll help you. I'll cook for you. I'll encourage you to exercise. I'll do everything I can to assist you in this thing."

He thinks he just expressed support, but what you may hear is, *You're fat and I do mind!*

HUSBAND'S RESPONSE OPTION #3

"You know, everybody's so into this weight thing for crying out loud. Everybody's talking about weight, weight, weight. What you weigh doesn't matter; it's about who you are as a person. Weight just doesn't matter!"

He thinks this put things into perspective, but what you may hear is, *You're not only fat—you also talk about dumb stuff!*

There may be times when nothing your husband says sounds right to you except maybe, "I don't know the right answer, but I love you!" And occasionally even that may not measure up to your need for affirmation.

Relating to each other is very complex, even for people who are trying to cooperate. Why should he be required to express his love to your specifications? If he is trying to say

he loves you in his way, don't let your frustration with yourself cause you to react poorly.

> *Listen for the best in*
> *your husband's responses.*

Listen for the best in your husband's responses. Much of the time difficulties of communication in a relationship are a result of selfishness. Strive less to be understood and try hard to understand.

> If you have any encouragement from being united with Christ, if any comfort from his love, if any fellowship with the Spirit, if any tenderness and compassion, then...do nothing out of selfish ambition or vain conceit, but in humility consider others better than yourselves...Look not only to your own interests, but also to the interests of others.
>
> —PHILIPPIANS 2:1–4

DO YOU THINK I WOULD WIN IF I WERE ON *SURVIVOR?*

Men ask interesting questions. There is something about being male—I think it must be the testosterone—that begs to compete and to conquer. One of the challenging things a wife may face as she communicates with her husband, is how to respond to his quest for success.

I know many women who meet this challenge well, and one of the best examples is my daughter-in-law Rhonda, who is just naturally amazing at this. Let me give you an example of one of her nearly flawless interchanges with her husband, Isaac.

"If I were on *Survivor*[4] do you think I would win?" Isaac asked over a bowl of popcorn. Rhonda responded with no hesitation. "Oh, I don't think so."

"What!? Why not?"

"Because, Isaac, you are so good at everything, they would know you would be the winner so they would try to vote you off right away so at least they could possibly have the chance to win."

Then Isaac smiled, and Rhonda did, too.

Rhonda has a gift. You may have it too, but maybe you aren't aware that you do because you hesitate to communicate with your husband in ways that encourage him. If you are capable of responding in positive, uplifting ways to friends, neighbors, or even strangers, then you have the same gift for encouraging that Rhonda has. All you have to do is expand your gift of positive, uplifting communication to include your husband.

If, however, you don't interact with anyone in this way, then it's time to meet the challenge and learn to do so. What Rhonda does almost instinctively, you can learn to do. Always use words that let your husband know that he is important to you and that you respect him.

> Like apples of gold in settings of silver is a word spoken in right circumstances.
> —PROVERBS 25:11, NASB

COMMUNICATION OPTIONS

If talking is one of your specialties, that's great, but don't limit yourself to that one way of communicating or you will miss some wonderful opportunities to connect with your husband. Gary Chapman's book, *The Five Love Languages— How to Express Heartfelt Commitment to Your Mate*[5] is an incredible resource for increasing effective communication in your marriage.

Chapman writes about five basic ways that you can give and receive love. Since love should be the basis of all communication with your husband, it is important to present information in the way that he can best receive it. The bottom line is, you will be most successful and encouraging in your communication with your husband if you figure out how he can best "hear" what you are saying and how you can best understand him. Quality time, words of affirmation, gifts, acts of service, and physical touch are all ways to communicate. *The Five Love Languages* can help you identify the best way to communicate with your husband.

WHO DO YOU SAY THAT YOU ARE?

All of that being said, the most powerful tool of communication you have at your disposal is your countenance. The love you have for God, the outlook you have on life, the ability you have to stay motivated and disciplined set a tone in your home. When your attitude and lifestyle are correct, the message you send to your husband is unmistakable: "I love you and I am bringing everything I can into this relationship to help you accomplish all that God has given us to do."

Every day do something to build your spirit, your mind, and your body. There is no need to compare your spirit to Mother Theresa's, your mind to Einstein's, or your body to that of a Greek goddess. Just take even a single step every day toward your desired destination of a better marriage, and you will be closer. You can only draw from what you have to offer, and God will continue to expand your capacity as you mature in each of these areas.

> From everyone who has been given much, much will be demanded; and from the one who has been entrusted with much, much more will be asked.
>
> —LUKE 12:48

CHAPTER SIX:
COMMUNICATION MATTERS

❧❧❧

MAKING IT PERSONAL

1. Name three things you do or don't do that may be causing problems in your communication with your husband.

    _____

    _____

    _____

2. Give some examples of specific things you can do (besides nag or clam up) when you don't get your desired response from your husband.

    _____

    _____

    _____

3. What are a few comments your husband makes to you that you might be able to consider in a more positive way than you normally do?

    _____

    _____

    _____

4. What is one positive way you know you can communicate with him without words?

    _____

5. List two ways you can improve your own countenance to offer a more positive message in your home.

    _____

    _____

CHAPTER SIX:
COMMUNICATION MATTERS

MAKING IT PRACTICAL

- Pray that your love for your husband will always be evident in your speech.

- Really listen when your husband talks and do not interrupt him.

- Read Scripture, get some exercise, and learn something new every day.

Blessing

*May you always communicate
the blessing that comes from knowing Jesus
Christ. And may knowing that God chose
you for your husband give you an enlarged sense of
purpose and make your marriage a celebration.*

With this in mind, we constantly pray for you, that our God may count you worthy of his calling, and that by his power *he may fulfill every good purpose of yours* and every act prompted by your faith.

—2 THESSALONIANS 1:11, EMPHASIS ADDED

Notes

INTRODUCTION
1. Jimmy Townsend, *It's True What They Say About Dixie* (Lakemont, GA: Copple House, 1981), as quoted at www.quoteproject.com, May 2001.

CHAPTER ONE: ENCOURAGEMENT
1. William Arthur Ward as quoted in *Apple Seeds,* compiled by Fr. Brian Cavanaugh (Third Order Franciscan), February 2000. This "quoteletter" is published through Franciscan University, Steubenville, Ohio, and is available at www.appleseeds.org.
2. Kevin A. Miller, "Marriage Partnership," *Marriage Partnership* magazine, fall 1996.
3. Whit Criswell, "First Steps to Happiness-Humility," *CBMC (Christian Business Men's Committee) Magazine,* 13 March 2000. Quote was obtained at www.cbmcint.org/manna/mm031300.html.
4. Carl Rogers, "Experiences in Communication," a lecture series at the California Institute of Technology (Pasadena, CA), 1964. A transcript of this lecture is available at www.aluvia.com/rogers2-eng.html.

CHAPTER TWO: SUBMISSION IMPOSSIBLE?
1. Helen Rowland as quoted by Robert Keeler, "The Toastmaster," *Readers' Digest,* June 1994, p. 130. Quote was obtained at www.sermonillustrations.com/a-z/m/marriage.htm, May 2001.
2. Lawrence O. Richards, *Expository Dictionary of Bible Words* (Grand Rapids, MI: Zondervan,1985), s.v. "desire."
3. *Wycliffe Bible Commentary,* Old Testament ed. Charles F. Pfeiffer (Chicago, IL: Moody Press, 1962), s.v. Genesis 2:18. Study of Genesis was written by Kyle M. Yates, Th.D., Ph.D., Professor of Old Testament, Baylor University, Waco, TX.
4. Ellen Goodman, "Ginger: America's High-Tech Sweetheart," 6 February 2001. The column was obtained at www.postwritersgroup.com.

CHAPTER THREE:
FINANCES

1. Crown's resources are available on the Internet at www.crown.org and through Christian bookstores.

CHAPTER FOUR:
SLEEPING TOGETHER

1. W. Stanley Mooneyham, *Come Walk the World* (Waco, TX: Word Books, 1978), as quoted in *Quotable Quotes, Wit and Wisdom for All Occasions,* ed. Deborah DeFord (Pleasantville, NY: Readers' Digest Associated Press, Inc., 1997).
2. Willard Harley, Jr., *His Needs, Her Needs,* (Old Tappan, NJ: Fleming H Revell, 1988), p.12.
3. Benjamin Franklin, *Poor Richard's Almanac* (1751), as quoted at www.sage-advice.com, May 2001.

CHAPTER FIVE:
PARENTAL TACTICS 101

1. Lillian Sparks, "Lillian's Touch," *Woman's Touch,* May/June 2000. *Woman's Touch* is an inspirational magazine for women published by the Assemblies of God USA.

CHAPTER SIX:
COMMUNICATION MATTERS

1. Information obtained from www.sermonillustrations.com/a-z/m/marriage.htm.
2. Stormie Omartian, *The Power of a Praying Wife* (Eugene, OR: Harvest House Publishers, 1997), p. 13.
3. Matthew Parris and Phil Mason, eds., *Read My Lips: A Treasury of the Things Politicians Wish They Hadn't Said* (NY: Robson Books, 1997), as quoted at www.teachingpsychology.com/archives/199909.html, May 2001.
4. Survivor is a TV reality game show in which a group of people is placed in some remote location of the planet and on several occasions, over a period of weeks, they vote to remove one individual from the group. The last person left in the remote location wins a million dollars.
5. Gary Chapman, *The Five Love Languages* (Chicago, IL: Moody Publishing, 1998).

About the Author

As a young girl, I prayed every night, "Lord, please protect my husband and let me know him when I see him." I believe God prompted me to pray that prayer. Many years later, He answered it.

The year I left for college, my home church hired Joel as a youth pastor. My two younger brothers, who were teens at the time, occasionally mentioned during phone conversations how great the new minister was.

During the fall break from classes, I attended worship at my home church. I was sitting between my boyfriend and my mother when I saw Joel walk down the center aisle in flowing pastoral robes. The moment I saw him, I knew God was showing me the husband that I had prayed for all those years. I had to tell someone, so I turned to my mother and said, "I'm going to marry him."

"Who?" she asked.

"That youth minister."

"Are you planning to tell your boyfriend?" she whispered with a grin.

"Not right now—and I'm not telling the youth minister either—not until after we are married."

"OK," she said, "then could you pass me that extra hymnal?"

Mom handled my announcement in stride. Nothing ever really rattled Mom. A teacher as well as a nurse, she had become unflappable. My father was equally solid. As a middle school principal who daily managed thousands of kids, he felt that raising my two brothers and me was a reprieve. I experienced a wonderful upbringing in a Christian home.

On Sunday, July 2, 1972, Joel and I were married. The day after our wedding, I told him that he was the answer to my childhood prayer. He still is—through a doctoral degree, three sons, four churches, seven residences, and wallpapering a ceiling together. He still is.

"The pastor's family lives in a fishbowl"—that's what I had always heard. Appreciating the droplet of truth in that, and knowing that as a Christian I should live in such a way that others might be drawn to Christ, I realized that I had an incredible possibility to witness for Him simply by the way I chose to live my daily life. Each member of our family personally recognized this as a special opportunity. As it says in Titus 2:7–8:

> In everything set them an example by doing what is good. In your teaching show integrity, seriousness and soundness of speech that cannot be condemned, so that those who oppose you may be ashamed because they have nothing bad to say about us.

Each season of marriage presented me with yet another opportunity to choose to be good to my husband on purpose. As a result, I have been a college student, stay-at-home mom, biology teacher, radio ministry administrator, and an editor of a church's weekly newspaper. Volunteer work in a variety of ministry efforts both inside and outside the church has broadened my perspective. All of these experiences have been satisfying, and most have taken place during our years of ministry at Northland, A Church Distributed.

Since 1985 Joel has served as the senior pastor of Northland, which is located in a suburb of Orlando, Florida. When we arrived from Indiana, our three sons were ten, eight, and four years of age. We began ministry to and with fewer than two hundred people who were attending worship services in the dilapidated roller rink they had recently purchased.

As time passed, our sons grew, and so did the church. Today two of our sons are married and in full-time ministry; one is single and in medical school. In 1998 we first learned the joy that comes with being grandparents. Presently, more than sixty-five hundred people worship at Northland at the seven identical worship services that are held each weekend in the renovated skating rink. Additionally, our children's classes minister to more than one thousand children during those worship services.

Northland is an evangelical, non-denominational, distributed church. The word *distributed* indicates that there is as much emphasis on ministry outside the walls of the building as there is on ministry inside those walls. The desire of the church is to bring people to maturity in Christ, and that maturity is ultimately demonstrated in ministry to others. To that end, Northland currently partners with many churches and ministry organizations. We are always looking for more opportunities to "support God's mission" and be good to others on purpose.

TO CONTACT
BECKY HUNTER

NORTHLAND,
A CHURCH DISTRIBUTED
530 Dog Track Road
Longwood, FL 32750

WEBSITE: www.northlandcc.net

PHONE: 407-830-7146

E-MAIL: joelswife@hotmail.com
or
becky.hunter@northlandcc.net